Give God a Chance

Ron R. McCatty

New Wine Press

New Wine Press
P.O. Box 17
Chichester
England PO20 6YB

Scripture quotations are from the King James Version
unless otherwise stated.

ISBN 0 0947852 98 0

Typeset by Falcon Typographic Art Ltd,
Fife, Scotland
Printed by Clays Ltd, Bungay, Suffolk

Contents

Foreword

Ron McCatty is a unique individual whose spiritual outlook has been moulded by his own experience of God. In the middle of a busy professional life he leads a lively Christian fellowship and so has a concern to see and say things clearly and to the point.

This book, GIVE GOD A CHANCE, is just what it says, an appeal and challenge to every believer to make room for God to move in greater reality and power in our life. The heart of the appeal is a call for us to depend utterly on God. The author doesn't like humbug and at times he cuts through what he sees to be falsehood and hypocrisy in the life and witness of the church at large. But his real concern is for a positive, open and loving response to God who has first made such overtures to our own hearts. He is for a passionate religion which manifests the reality and power of God.

The book draws upon much Biblical inspiration and example and through its pages walk again the great men and women of God from the Scriptures. This is true of none more than Elijah who comes through as the great inspiration to prayer and commitment. The effectiveness of Elijah's cry to

God and his persistence before God and men present us with a profound challenge with regard to the shallowness of much of our own faith. Each chapter highlights another important key to spiritual power and effectiveness in our own lives.

This clear challenge to commitment is sounded, at times, within a context of a warning. The author has little time for what he sees as the false call for unity at large in much social and religious life today. In fact, he sees it as one of the hallmarks of the end times and he warns us against imbibing the spirit of the age in which we live.

'To be filled with the Spirit then is to be filled with God, a revolutionary mighty experience that warms up the coldest heart.' Words like these highlight the central message of this book and who can doubt that this is exactly what we all need today. We need to GIVE GOD A CHANCE!

(Bob Gordon, Director, Kerygma Christian Trust, Drayton Hall Christian Centre, Norwich. U.K.)

Chapter 1

Prayer Equals Power!

There has never been a day when the need for prayer warriors was greater. This is probably the greatest lack in the Church currently, – men and women of faith who are really 'violent' in prayer, and who will not quit when the answer is not immediate.

One of the most striking results of the outpouring of the Holy Spirit upon the early Christian Church was their devotion to prayer. They had their priorities sorted out, announcing: *'We will give ourselves continually to prayer . . .'* (Acts 6:4).

That word 'continually' was significant. They prayed when it was convenient and when it was not, in their homes, on the streets, in their meetings, in times of distress, in storms and out of storms, in prisons and outside of prisons. Their prayers affected towns and cities, villages and every stratum of society. Like their Master, Jesus, had done just before them, the disciples 'went out' into the world empowered by the Holy Spirit, seeking the lost, and they did not need 'Specialist leaders and teachers' to help them. They were dynamic and effective. The Holy Spirit was in charge. Possessing an irrepressible evangelistic zeal, they were successful both in prayer and ministry.

When they prayed earthquakes erupted, buildings shook, prisoners' chains fell apart and gaolers cried out for mercy. There were no hit or miss prayers in those days. They were anointed and specific. They were costly, heart searching and effective.

Talking about costly, let us not forget Gethsemane. The prayer that our Saviour uttered there was priceless. He was facing crucifixion and would pray as no one had ever done or will ever do.

The weight of the sin of the whole world was upon His shoulders. As the mental and spiritual anguish heightened to an almost unbearable level Jesus cried out *'Father, if thou be willing, remove this cup from me: nevertheless not my will, but thine, be done'* (Luke 22:42). I believe in that agonizing cry He was giving vent to the awful spectre of His not enduring to arrive at Calvary's Cross to accomplish His immense mission of dying for our sins. I also believe that His cry was an expression of humanity. *'And being in an agony he prayed more earnestly: and his sweat was as it were great drops of blood falling down to the ground.'*

We shall never know the depth, height, or breadth of His agony. We shall never know the measure of His sacrifice in Gethsemane or on Calvary's Cross. We are not required to, but we do know that He did all that was needful. As 1 Peter 3:18 says, *'For Christ also hath once suffered for sins, the just for the unjust, that He might bring us to God, being put to death in the flesh, but quickened by the spirit.'* In those final moments of immense pressure on one hand, but also wonderful triumph over the Devil and sin, Jesus exclaimed *'it is finished!'*

Those were perhaps the greatest words ever uttered on earth, as the most effective prayer warrior of all time *'bowed his head, and gave up the Ghost.'* Luke 23:34 & 46 record the last two days of Jesus' prayers: *'Father, forgive them; for they know not what they do.'* This was in regard of those who were directly responsible for His Crucifixion *'And when Jesus had cried with a loud voice, he said, Father, into thy hands I commend my spirit.'* Jesus' whole life was one of prayer, even to the last moment as we have seen, and the legacy that He has left us is inestimable. When we consider John 17, it is a marvel; one of the most beautiful passages in the whole Bible: a prayer for us. There He commits us into the hands of the Father, and how powerful that really is!

On leaving this earth the resurrected Saviour promised and has sent power that the Apostles and all who follow in their steps may carry on from where He left off. He would have His Church empowered by the Holy Spirit, to pray as He did.

The English word, dynamite, derives from the Greek word 'dunamis' meaning power. That was what the first Christian Church had, power par excellence. Once they had received that heavenly boost from on high on the day of Pentecost, their timidity, fear and lack of confidence were instantly banished. Those men of God were transformed into precious warriors of the Cross of Christ. They *'went about'* even as it is written of their Lord, Jesus. They went in the power of the Holy Spirit, being anointed of God and accomplishing supernatural works in the name of Jesus.

9

Their witness was not only real, but effective. It is this power and effectiveness that is so urgently needed in the Church at present. There is no lack of the preaching of truth. Neither is there any shortage of eloquent and even well trained preachers. Many evangelical churches are well endowed with these. In some, their congregations appear large and happy. There is nothing to say against that, but an examination of their spiritual standing/power can be very alarming; and what is the criterion for this examination? The Scriptures, of course! Let us not forget that the truth on its own, though indispensable, is not enough, *'For the letter killeth'* says the Bible, *'but the Spirit giveth life.'* In many circles the unspoken emphasis is on dignity, at the cost of humility and prayer. Neither is there any clamour after the power from on high, which would sweep away all the stuffiness and spiritual ignorance to the exalting of Jesus Christ. So many cling to their sophisticated, dignified, yet ineffective religiosity. There is blissful disregard for the wonder-working power of Pentecost, that transcending heavenly dimension which made the early Christians so bold and distinguishable for their God.

Currently there are some folk teaching that the supernatural was for that day only, the apostles' day. That is blind ignorance. The only hope for the Christian Church is for a spiritual awakening, on the lines of Joel 2:28, for example. On the day of Pentecost Peter was so excited about that spiritual 'breakthrough' from heaven that recalling this that Joel had prophesied, he shouted *'this is that . . .'* But it is our belief that the best is yet to be! Spiritual ignorance and apathy must be cleared out of the church.

The imminent return of Jesus Christ is the Christian's expectation, and there is an anticipated massive harvest of souls just before that for His Kingdom. It is the Holy Spirit who will accomplish this through God's praying people. Already many are enjoying His reign and lead in their lives both individually and collectively. Yet still, the urgent need of the moment is for a people who are imbued with a Divine passion *'to pray, and not to faint'* (Luke 18:1). This is not just a church matter. It concerns every one of us, every man, woman and child on the street, in the homes, factories, schools and everywhere else, for God has spoken. He says in 2 Chron. 7:14 *'If my people, which are called by my name, shall humble themselves, and pray, and seek my face, and turn from their wicked ways; then will I hear from heaven, and will forgive their sin, and will heal their land.'* Does this land need healing?

The answer to that question must be that it certainly does. Violence is increasing at an alarming rate. Murders are commonplace; rape, burglary, theft, mugging, and the beating up of old people are every-day occurrences. We have almost got used to major disasters too. The Zeebrugge incident for example, cyclones in Bangladesh, the Pan Am aircrash/sabotage, earthquakes in America and Russia, gigantic storms in Europe, volcanic eruptions in the Philippines . . . there is nowhere that is not affected.

And what of our institutions? The hospitals are

11

full, and so are the prisons. Law and order are despised. Anarchy stalks our streets, cities and towns. Custodial sentences are practically meaningless and our police officers are objects of derision and contempt. No one appears to have the power or authority to stem the rapid breakdown in society. What can we do? Pray!

There is a cry going up to God. There are people crying out for help, and God will send His answer not only to their quest, but to the world's dilemma. We must continue in prayer. He has not abandoned His people. Zephaniah 3:17 is encouraging. *'The Lord thy God in the midst of thee is mighty; he will save, he will rejoice over thee with joy; he will rest in his love, he will joy over thee with singing.'*

Some might have thought that God is not interested, that He does not care after all. But let us listen to what He says. The present state of things around us is all in the plan for revival; God's plan. Nothing is happening by chance *'and all things are of God . . .'* (2 Cor. 5:17.18). Many people are apt to blame the Devil for much more than they ought. They appear to think that he is responsible for the state of the world or that there is some big contest going on right now, which is God versus the Devil. It is certainly not so. There is no such contest. Whose Devil is he anyhow? He is God's, and can only do what he is allowed. There are numerous references in Scripture to support this. For example in Isaiah 45:7 we read that God says *'I form the light, and create darkness: I make peace, and create evil: I the Lord do all these things.'*

There is also the story of that wonderful Old Testament character, Job. The Devil appeared before God one day and God asked him how he was getting on, and from where was he coming just then. In reply the Devil/Satan said *'from going to and fro in the earth, and from walking up and down in it.'* The Lord then asked him if he had considered His *'servant Job, that there is none like him in the earth, a perfect and an upright man, one that feareth God, and escheweth evil?'* (Job 1:8). The Devil told God that he was of the opinion that Job's respect for Him was only because God was protecting him, and blessing all his possessions; but if He withdrew His support, Job would curse Him to His face. *'And the Lord said unto Satan, behold all that he hath is in thy power, only upon himself put not forth thine hand.'*

It was from then that Satan went from the presence of the Lord and started harassing Job. There was disaster after disaster in that man's life. He lost everything he had, and that was a lot, for he was the richest man around in those days. We will not major on Job's catastrophes right now, as the real point we are illustrating is simply that God is in everything, however bad it might appear to be. Let it be emphasised that it was God who gave the Devil leave to attack Job, and he certainly did. There are tremendous pressures right now upon God's people. They are meant to feel them. The greater the pressures the greater the response to God, the cry to Him for help. God loves us too much to let us be independent of Him. There is no need for dismay, only prayer.

The Anointing Will Make The Difference

When we read a passage such as Haggai 2:6 it gives us courage to press on, *'For thus saith the Lord of hosts; Yet once, it is a little while, and I will shake the heavens, and the earth, and the sea, and the dry land; And I will shake all nations, and the desire of all nations shall come: and I will fill this house with glory, saith the Lord of hosts.'* Is there a shaking of the nations today? Are men's hearts failing them for the pressures that are coming upon them? The answers to these questions are obvious and need no explanation. It is time for God's people to *'look up'* warns Jesus, *'for their redemption draweth nigh.'* It is also time to pray and not to be slack about it. The shaking is purposeful, *'that those things which cannot be shaken, may remain'* (Heb. 12:27). The 'Desire' of all nations is coming soon. The disciples were first called Christians at Antioch (Acts 11:26); why were they? Obviously because they lived like Christ. They walked and talked like Him, manifested His love and holiness, and prayed like Him, – effectively.

From the evidence we have in Scripture then, for modern Christians to be really effective they must be a people who are anointed and led by the Holy Spirit. In this sense there is no difference between male and female. *'For as many as are led by the Spirit of God, they are the sons of God'* (Rom. 8:14). They are *'a chosen generation, a royal priesthood, an holy nation, a peculiar people;'* chosen by God to appear before Him with priestly concerns (see 1 Peter 2:9). Knowing their calling and mission they are zealous and pray with a godly fervour that is always effective.

There is a special dignity about the spirit-filled persons who live in accord with the Word of God. They enjoy 'the liberty' of sonship, seizing upon every opportunity to pray fervently, as though it were the last hour. They are also like Aaron of old, the priest of the Lord. Exodus 28:12 shows him bearing two stones in the shoulders of his ephod bejewelled with the names of the children of Israel set in gold. What a precious picture of a prayer warrior that is, a person called out and anointed of God bearing up his brethren before the Lord!

It is vital for modern Christians to be praying like that, bearing up others before God, putting His interests first: that is effectiveness. There are many praying but the challenge remains, are they praying effectively? It is not left to us as to whether we are effective. As we make ourselves available to God He in turn makes Himself available to us and empowers us with His Spirit to be the people we ought to be before Him. God's power is available to every prayer warrior that he/she might be in constant communion with Him, that His will may be done on earth as it is in heaven. The words they use do not appear to matter very much.

What seems to be an imperative ingredient is the motive. If God's interest is paramount, *'the zeal of the Lord of Hosts will perform it.'* That is exactly how it was with Jesus. He was infused with holy zeal, the zeal of *'The Lord of Hosts,'* and did only those things that were pleasing to God.

You can always tell when people are praying hit or miss prayers, I mean prayers which are not motivated

15

by the Holy Spirit. They are praying what they think necessary, and are usually a little worldly wise, ending such prayers with 'if it be thy will, Lord.' One does not have to be very spiritual to realise that such prayers are ineffective and unanswerable. In the matter of praying for the sick, with some this lack of confidence is particularly noticeable. There is no expression of faith or assurance in their prayers. The Bible says *'whatsoever is not of faith is sin.'* Might not their good intentions then be a way of sinning rather than blessing?

Jesus taught in the Gospels that when we pray we must believe that we receive the things for which we pray, and then we shall have them. It must be remembered that He was speaking as the Anointed One, a man led entirely by the Holy Spirit. Acts 10:38 tells us *'How God anointed Jesus of Nazareth with the Holy Ghost and with power: who went about doing good, and healing all that were oppressed by the devil; for God was with him.'*

From this text we must conclude that Jesus could not help being effective in His ministry and relationship with God the Father because of the anointing with the Holy Ghost and with power. Once having received this precious gift, this heavenly endowment, it was the very presence of God who neither left nor forsook Him. Speaking no doubt from experience, Jesus says in John 16 that *'when he, the Spirit of truth, is come, he will guide you into all truth.'* How comprehensive! *'For,'* continues Jesus, *'He shall not speak of himself; but whatsoever he shall hear, that shall he speak: and he will show you things to come.'*

16

Chapter 2

Elijah –
Rising to the Challenge

Jesus' words in John 16 are very encouraging. How marvellous that the Spirit of Truth shall guide us into all truth! Surely this is the guarantee that God's end time people must be an effective people, indeed herald's of Jesus' imminent return. The Holy Spirit showing us things to come would involve showing us the things that are in God's heart about which we must pray at this time. That was exactly what he used to do for Jesus. Hence Jesus' testimony, *'The Son can do nothing of himself, but what he seeth the Father do: for what things soever he doeth, these also doeth the Son likewise'* (John 5:19).

Speaking of effectiveness, in James 5:16 it is recorded *'The effectual fervent prayer of a righteous man availeth much.'* A righteous person would quite naturally be one of faith and substance in God. In himself he might be quite ordinary, not standing head and shoulders above others in world affairs, but he would have a sound relationship with his God.

James is careful to give us an example of a righteous man in case we think we are not righteous when we already are. *'Our righteousness is of God'.*

James speaks of a man called Elias. He explains that Elias was an ordinary person like any of us, one of emotions and fears. He ate, slept, snored in his sleep perhaps, had masculine feelings, laughed and joked like anybody else, yet there was something particular about him. He had power with God. In James' own words, *'Elias was a man subject to like passions as we are, and he prayed earnestly that it might not rain: and it rained not on the earth by the space of three years and six months. And he prayed again, and the heaven gave rain, and the earth brought forth her fruit.'*

That is the calibre of man to whom God is looking, one who has the ear of his Saviour, and who will pray according *to* His will rather than, *if it be* His will. It is well worth recalling the incident that prompted James' writing about Elias in this way. The record is in 1 Kings 17–18. Ahab the King was a wicked person, promoting idolatry in the land. *'He did more to provoke the Lord God of Israel to anger than all the Kings of Israel that were before him'* (1 Kings 16:33).

No one seemed even remotely concerned or brave enough to question the increasing tide of ungodliness in the land. But at the beginning of Chapter 17 we see a man emerging with the name Elijah, who is in fact, Elias, a man of prayer. He was a godly person and being utterly repulsed by King Ahab's behaviour he was not afraid to say so. He stood up against Ahab and rebuked him for his idolatry, saying something like this. 'Look, King Ahab, this is enough. You have ruined our country through the worship of Baalim. There is nothing to be gained from this, only poverty, confusion and shame, for the wrath of God has settled upon this land. You are the main trouble in this nation . . . You and your ungodly family. Someone has to put a stop to this nonsense and it might as well be myself.'

'As the Lord God of Israel liveth, before whom I stand, there shall not be dew nor rain these years, but according to my word' (1 Kings 17:1).

That was no simple rebuke; and hardly a prayer some of us might say. Granted it might not seem like prayer but it was the result of communion with God. It was, as we have already seen accepted by James, that Elijah prayed earnestly. That must be good enough. That prophet was a man whose life was given over to the Almighty. Recall what he said of his position in relation to God, *'before whom I stand.'* Elijah was sure of his stance before the Almighty. In times of crises some Christians don't really know where they stand, and this is not surprising if they are not living a life of prayer. By the very confidence Elijah displayed in his rebuke of the King it was obvious that he was in communion with God. Can you imagine him getting through a day without praying, without talking with his God?

Immediately after this episode God told Elijah to do something that would be an even bigger test of his faith and trust in Him. He told him to go and hide himself away, by the brook Cherith. You and I might think, well, why had he to do that? Couldn't God have provided him with protection just where he was? Surely the King, though very much insulted and humiliated by Elijah, could have been kept from retaliating? That is all true, but not necessarily important. The life of a man of prayer is not one of ease. It must be exposed to warfare. We must be kept in exercise, spiritual exercise. This becomes easier to understand when we realise that Cherith means, 'place of cutting'. Might it not be that Elijah was being 'cut down to size,' being prepared for accomplishing mighty acts of power?

The hiding that Elijah had to do was no simple matter, by that brook close to Jordan, a dirty river. Could there have been a better place for prayer exercise? Here, according to God he should stay and drink from the brook, and as though that was not enough, God further informed him that He had issued another command, but this time not to him, but to a certain bird of prey, *'the ravens to feed him there.'*

It is difficult to imagine how Elijah felt at that time after hearing all that, but it is worthy of note that he instantly obeyed. That was not natural obedience. Had it been, he would not have had the ability to receive the command. The apostle Paul in 1 Cor. 2:14 says *'the natural man receiveth not the things of the Spirit of God: for they are foolishness unto him: neither can he know them, because they are spiritually discerned.'*

On arrival at Cherith, Elijah received his food twice daily, morning and evening, by 'air' delivery, and he duly 'drank' from the brook. It is not recorded that in a little while he had dysentery, typhoid or any other disease as a result of dietary indiscretion. As a matter of fact he drank of that brook until it ran dry. That is what the Bible says. He did not appear to complain about anything. He must really have prayed over his water and food! They were truly sanctified. Considering Elijah's drinking, one cannot help being reminded of that passage in Mark's gospel, chapter 16, where Jesus in His farewell speech says that *these signs shall follow them that believe; in my name shall they cast out devils . . . and if they drink any deadly thing, it shall not hurt them.*' How could it? He is praying for them. This is how He speaks to God the Father on their behalf according to John 17:9: *'I pray not for the world, but for them which thou hast given me; for they are thine.*'

This should be most comforting to us that our Saviour Jesus is in constant prayer for us. Even at the risk of appearing indulgent it is well worth lingering over this matter for a moment.

The entire chapter, John 17, is a glowing account of how much Jesus loves and cares for us. He is not ashamed to own us, *'they are mine.*' Every Christian should read that with thanksgiving to the Lord. Elijah did not have this type of thing to sustain him. We do not read of anyone praying for him or supporting him in any way. This is not to say he lacked anything that was necessary for his personal needs or his mission as prophet, but on those days when everything seems topsy-turvy, it is always a wonderful safety net to be able to reflect on the fact that it is written in God's last Will and Testament that Jesus is actually praying for us.

Jesus Himself took advantage of the availability of the written Word in times of crises. When He was being tempted by the Devil to engage in inconvenient pursuits, *'it is written,'* was His strong point. For Him that was His weapon *'the Sword of the Spirit,'* against the Enemy. By this Jesus overcame him and came out of that situation unscathed, victorious indeed.

Three years after Elijah's memorable encounter with King Ahab, God spoke to him: *'Go, show thyself unto Ahab; and I will send rain upon the earth'* (1 Kings 18:1). By this time there was chaos in the land. Everything was in short supply because of the long drought, and not surprisingly Mrs Ahab (Jezebel) had executed the Lord's prophets, as many as she could find. It is certainly not difficult to understand why she had done this. As far as she was concerned, taking Elijah as an example, prophets of the Lord were dangerous people. They prayed, and their prayers had very positive effects, even to the causing of economic paralysis to a whole nation. They had to be eliminated.

Most of the animals had already died from starvation and thirst. Industry was at a standstill: *'there was a sore famine in Samaria.'* Humanly speaking this was surely the worst time possible for Elijah to face Ahab. Generally, things were bad before Elijah rebuked him, but since that time they had become very much worse.

Could not God have arranged some more convenient time or place for Elijah to call on the King who was now his angry enemy? Might it not have been better for these two men to meet on neutral ground? Obviously not. David in the Psalms very aptly warns us that God's ways are not like ours; nor are His thoughts; they are much higher and different. Elijah's pending contest with Ahab was also God's, as subsequent events were conclusively to prove.

Having regard for the economic plight that was biting into the nation, Ahab called up one of his chief ministers, Obadiah, a good man, a minister of religion whom he trusted. He was the one who was responsible for looking after the Royal household. They discussed the gravity of the situation *'and Ahab said unto Obadiah go into the land, unto all fountains of water, and unto all brooks peradventure we may find grass to save the horses and mules alive, that we lose not all the beasts. So they divided the land between them to pass throughout it: Ahab went one way by himself, and Obadiah went another way by himself.'* They had not gone very far when Obadiah met Elijah who was possibly on his way to the palace to see the King, as God commanded.

Was that a chance meeting? What do you think?

The Bible says the steps of a good man are ordered by the Lord. We have already established the 'pedigree' of both Elijah and Obadiah. They were men of experience with God, praying men; men of spiritual substance, good men. It is recorded in the Scriptures that *'Obadiah feared the Lord greatly'* and when Jezebel was executing the Lord's prophets Obadiah rescued one hundred of them, *'and hid them by fifty in a cave, and fed them with bread and water.'* Given the famine circumstances of the time, it is possible that was the best that was available in the way of food for those prophets, but as to hiding them that was another matter. We shall come back to this later.

Overcoming Authority

Hardly had Elijah and Obadiah exchanged greetings when Elijah said to him *'go, and tell thy lord, Behold Elijah is here.'* 'Oh, no,' he said, 'I am not going to do that. That is the easiest way for me to be killed by Ahab. He has been searching everywhere for you in every "nation or Kingdom" I know your type, Elijah. The moment I tell Ahab that you are here *"the Spirit of the Lord shall carry thee whither I know not; and so when I come and tell Ahab, and he cannot find thee, he shall slay me:"* Definitely not! I cannot do it Elijah!' Elijah was not daunted. Man of destiny that he was, he simply girded up his spiritual loins, as it were, and made a positive confession similar to the one which he had made to Ahab earlier when invoking the drought *'as the Lord of Hosts liveth, before whom I stand, I will surely shew myself unto Him today.'*

Note that after the three years had elapsed Elijah was still announcing that he was standing before 'The Lord of Hosts' and had not lost any ground. How significant that was!

I believe Elijah was saying to the enemy, 'note that I am fully backed by the One who cannot fail. Make way for Him, He is Lord of Lords; Lord of Hosts of men and nations, Lord of Hosts of angels, birds, animals . . .' He was confessing what was in his heart; his testimony which so beautifully accords with Rev. 12:11; *'And they overcame* (the enemy) *by the blood of the Lamb, and by the word of their testimony.'*

At last Ahab met Elijah, and as we might imagine was instantly on the offensive. 'Are you the one who has wrecked our country he demanded aggressively?' 'Oh, no;' replied Elijah, *"I have not troubled Israel."* You are the culprit. You, and your entire family, *"in that ye have forsaken the commandments of the Lord, and thou hast followed Baalim."*

What a challenge that was! It is time to pray that God might raise up men like Elijah in our day. How many Christians do we hear of standing up to the government and saying, look, you have forsaken the laws of the Lord God? You are worshipping at the shrine of materialism. You are bowing down at the altar of science and technology, of education, politics and philosophy: what about turning to the Almighty for a change? Give God a chance!

If ever we needed people of prayer and faith in the land it is now. We also need the voice of the prophet in our nation. The prophet in Scripture is always associated with recovery, a return to godliness. God raised up a prophetess in the person of Deborah to inspire Barak (Judges 4:4). More recently He raised up John Wesley, George Muller, Smith Wigglesworth . . . and as we pray He will raise up a people today attesting to His love, majesty and power, – a people of prayer. Some of our modern prophets prophesy what people want to hear, but here is what makes the difference. God's prophets prophesy what God wants to say to people. Like Elijah, Deborah was living in a loftier place positively with God. A woman of prayer – she was in constant victory, hence her inspiring faith.

Speaking again of 'recovery' we must take a further look at Elijah. His latter condemnation of Ahab, his family and Baalim, was to play a very significant role in the overthrow of idolatry. *'Now therefore'* said Elijah, *'send, and gather to me all Israel unto Mount Carmel, and the prophets of Baal four hundred and fifty, and the prophets of the groves four hundred, which eat at Jezebel's table.'*

It must be born in mind that Elijah was, naturally speaking, no more than a subject of the realm. But by the way he spoke to the King, we could almost think the reverse was the truth. The prophet's authority was unquestionable. His poise as a man of God was indomitable. His authority was supreme. It is worth reading those verses in 1 Kings 18:19–20 to see how obedient King Ahab had become to that man of God. Verse 20 says *'So Ahab sent unto all the children of Israel, and gathered the prophets together unto Mount Carmel.'* I wonder what the King was thinking as he did all this. The Bible does not say anything of that, but it is plain that he recognised higher authority, especially as *'Elijah came unto all the people, and said, How long halt ye between two opinions? If the Lord be God, follow Him: but if Baal, then follow him.'*

Under the tyranny of Ahab the law of the land was that Baalim was the god to be worshipped. The people were not convinced that that was correct. They had great leanings toward God Almighty. After all He was originally the God of Israel, but now as we have seen, apart from Elijah no one had raised a note of objection to the idolatry; there was a general malaise.

Even Obadiah had kept quiet, possibly in order to hold onto his job. We don't know how much of an accolade he deserves for hiding those one hundred prophets at such a critical time. Who can tell, if they had been encouraged to be out and about prophesying what God wanted people to hear, Jezebel might have been thwarted in her evil work. And we may question whether as a man of God he had any right to join forces with Ahab albeit in search of water. Can two who are not in agreement walk together? Can light mix with darkness?

Having a leaning toward God is certainly not one and the same thing as worshipping Him. Therefore God's man on the spot, the 'remnant' in the person of Elijah, raised the challenge for people to stand up and be counted. The time had come for them to declare themselves either for God or not. Elijah would have this matter sorted out. One is immediately reminded of Moses of old, as he led the rebellious multitude through the wilderness. He was tired of their half-heartedness, and when he had pitched the tent outside the camp he demanded that those who were on the Lord's side should make it known by leaving the congregation for the tent. The Church of Jesus Christ is facing the same kind of thing today. In Christendom there is certainly a choice to be made, a definite choice. The same Holy Spirit that motivated Moses and Elijah those thousands of years ago is at work right now sorting out God's people!

Chapter 3

Special Mission

This chapter is about mission or assignment. Elijah was a man with a mission. There is a desperate shortage of men like him, a shortage of men of God; men with a God-given mission: men like Muller, Spurgeon, Wigglesworth, of the not-too-distant past.

Today we have Christian churches, Christian Projects, Christian teaching, Christian doctrine, theology and philosophy but Christianity in the first place is none of these. We have ceremony, we have liturgy, but Christianity is not a system, not a label nor a doctrine. It is a living person, Christ the Lord. The Holy Spirit wants to exalt Him the Chief Corner Stone, which once the builders rejected. So God would put His Spirit upon His people to this end that the Son of His delight might be lifted up, and seen as He really is.

People with a mission from God are special to Him, and are specially equipped for particular tasks. They are motivated by His Spirit to be His 'witnesses.' Elijah is a tremendous example of this, and according to Jesus our Saviour, the spirit and power of Elijah will be manifestly in the Church during the last days making a people ready for His personal return (Matt. 11:12–15). The last chapter of Malachi accords with these words of Jesus.

Elijah was highly spiritually motivated. A man of destiny, he was dynamic and effective. That mount Carmel episode was a masterpiece, something over which we would do well to ponder. When we consider how thorough the overthrow of idolatry in Israel was, and what that must have meant to God, it is really remarkable. It is the type of thing that every Christian should covet to bring about in his or her own land today.

It is evident from the Scriptures that some people are specially called. Many say times have changed, that we are living in a completely different day from Elijah's; but I contend that God has not changed, and surely He hates idolatry no less now than He did then.

Idolatry has not lessened in gravity or in the number of people engaging in it. There are more people worshipping their own gods today than ever before, to the exclusion of God Almighty. We have already reviewed these matters in an earlier chapter. In this chapter it is intended in particular that we might see from the Scriptures the bearing that Elijah's ministry is meant to have on Christianity in our time. Such a ministry I believe is meant to illustrate the effects of the anointing that was to come upon the New Testament Church.

John the Baptist was the last of the Old Testament prophets. It is rather curious how his life began and just as curious how it ended so quickly in about 30 years. This is how it began: in Luke 1 we see God's angel advising an old couple, Zacharias and Elizabeth, that they were going to have a son. These people had faithfully served God for years, Zacharias being a devout priest; but there was something wrong. His wife 'was barren.' According to verse 13, she and her husband had prayed much about her state, as they had so longed for children. The evidence that God had heard them was now to hand! His angel had called on Zacharias with the wonderful news, *'thy prayer is heard; and thy wife Elizabeth shall bear thee a son, and thou shalt call his name John. And thou shalt have joy and gladness; and many shall rejoice at his birth. For he shall be great in the sight of the Lord, and shall drink neither wine nor strong drink; and shall be filled with the Holy Ghost, even from his mothers womb.'*

What an assignment! What a mission! So even before John was born his lifestyle was ordained by God, his being 'filled with the Holy Ghost' equipped indeed to do the work which God intended that he should do. No doubt this gives us some understanding of the background of the Old Testament prophets in general, as to why they were so mighty in word and deed. They were specially equipped and did not choose their own work. It was chosen for them and they were commissioned by God.

Nevertheless, in many respects John was different from the majority of his predecessors. What the angel had said to Zacharias was a declaration of the type of person he was going to be – unique.

The significance of that declaration was that he would be the forerunner of Jesus. He would prepare the way for Him. That was going to be a tremendous responsibility, which could never be left to a merely natural human being, but to one of the Spirit – a man 'filled'. It certainly needed someone who would work in a different dimension. The text shows that John would go before the Lord in the spirit and power of Elias. This he would do to make the fathers and children agree and the disobedient change their lifestyle to the correct way of living . . . that there should be a general preparedness for the coming of the Lord.

That was a special assignment which no one before him had ever received. It is particularly interesting to see in verse 15 that the Lord would see John as a special person. This was confirmed by the compliment Jesus paid him in His preaching *'For I say unto you among those that are born of women there is not a greater prophet than John the Baptist . . .'* (Luke 7:28).

When John was born it was an occasion of tremendous rejoicing. The Bible says Elizabeth's *'neighbours and her cousins heard how the Lord had showed great mercy upon her; and they rejoiced with her,'* just as the angel had foretold when he informed Zacharias that his prayer was heard. By the time of John's dedication some eight days later, his parents were well aware of God's favour being upon their very young child. *'And his father Zacharias was filled with the Holy Ghost,'* at the dedication *'and prophesied, saying . . . and thou, child, shalt be called the prophet of the Highest: for thou shalt go before the face of the Lord to prepare his ways; to give knowledge of salvation unto his people by the remission of their sins.'* (Luke 1.67–77). How confirming that was of all that had been said of him less than a year earlier, when no one but God even knew what his appearance would be, whether he would be dark or fair, round faced or whatever!

Not surprisingly John emerged as one of the greatest preachers of all time. *'Then said he to the multitude that came forth to be baptized of him. O generation of vipers, who hath warned you to flee from the wrath to come? Bring forth therefore fruits worthy of repentance . . .'* And they did. Even Pharisees and publicans forsook their way of life and embraced John's message of repentance, so powerful was his ministry. Imagine any of our preachers like this one calling his congregation a brood of snakes. No doubt we would be a little more discreet with our analogies, but not John. He had no reason to be. It was the Spirit of the Lord who had taken hold upon him for speaking as he did. There was supernatural power in his words. When the Spirit is in charge there is no reason to suspect the worst. In such circumstances some of the things that we would not normally say are often correct for the occasions when we say them.

We cannot do justice to discussing John and his being filled with the Spirit for his special mission, without considering Jesus our Lord and His filling with the same Holy Spirit for the supreme mission of doing His Father's will. The record is in Matt. 3:16. It shows how the Holy Spirit descended upon Him at the river Jordan, as He came up out of the water, having been baptized by John. The text says *'and Jesus, when he was baptized, went up straightway out of the water: and, lo, the heavens were opened unto him, and he saw the Spirit of God descending like a dove, and lighting upon him.'* That was marvellous! Even He had to be filled with the Spirit.

Before we proceed let us read in another of the Gospels Jesus confirming that He had received this special endowment. Luke 4:14 shows Him returning *'in the power of the Spirit into Galilee'* after a tremendous crisis, which involved Him in a very grave temptation with the Devil.

Jesus went on to His home town, *'Nazareth, where he had been brought up: and, as his custom was, he went into the synagogue on the Sabbath day, and stood up for to read.'* The book of Esaias was handed to Him by the minister and on opening it He began to read *'The Spirit of the Lord is upon me, because he hath anointed me to preach the gospel to the poor; he hath sent me to heal the broken hearted . . .'* This was obviously not long after His experience at Jordan, and now He was at pains to stress that what He had received there was that particular anointing for His ministry, as was prophesied by Esaias. And what a comprehensive ministry that was going to be! As we have already seen, John's turned out to be great, in fact very great, although his was but preparatory. The ministry of all ministries was to be found in Jesus the Lord.

Nevertheless, John was so effective in all that he did that people were questioning whether he was the Christ. *'John answered, saying unto them all, I indeed* baptize you with water; but One mightier than I cometh, the latchet of whose shoes I am not worthy to unloose: He shall baptize you with the Holy Ghost and with fire' (Luke 3:16). There was no competition, was there? No, not even a nuance of it. John knew who he was and confessed 'I am not the Christ' (John 1:20). He was not slow to tell that someone mightier than he was on the way.

John would not be goaded into making any claims about himself, as far as he was concerned he was just 'the voice of one crying in the wilderness, Prepare ye the way of the Lord, and make His paths straight.' Possessed of the Holy Spirit what else could he have said? The words that he was using were both of and by the Spirit who stands for nothing less than the exaltation of Christ.

Not for volunteers
A man with a mission then should know at least three things in particular – his saviour – Christ the Lord, the Scriptures and himself. This is not an automatic appreciation of salvation, but diligence regarding the things of God will always be enhanced by the presence of the Holy Spirit. A person with a mission is either born to it or drawn to it, specially chosen, anointed and appointed by God. All through the Scriptures this is evident. Yet so many who go out as missionaries or full-time evangelists finish up disheartened or disillusioned. Might the problem be that they were not chosen?

I think of a man I know whose lifestyle illus- trates the point. He was an evangelist – self-styled perhaps? I knew him very well. Before he 'felt' the mission-call upon his life he had been a successful farmer. Leaving that aside he took on the mantle of the prophet, preacher and teacher in the name of Christ, and became very popular. No one could gainsay his ministry. There were the 'signs following' just as the Scriptures say they would for the one who believes (Mark 16:17). This buoyant ministry continued for a year or two. Then latterly it became evident that wherever this man went he was leaving a trail of debts and ill-will. Obviously his way of living was not in accord with the ministry. It should be no surprise today that that dear brother is now thoroughly disillusioned, disappointed, distraught and back in secular employment.

Mission is a calling from God. It requires the individual's entire involvement, and that originates in heaven. God is choosy as to the people He equips and commissions for His work. A good example of this is Saul of Tarsus. God chose him, a most unlikely person, a notorious religious fanatic. A Pharisee above Pharisees, Saul had committed and was still committing horrendous atrocities against God's people. Mercilessly persecuting and harassing those Christians, he committed many to a life of misery and torment.

If you or I had been given the task of selecting someone for the ministry, Saul of Tarsus would never have come into our minds, or even if he had, we would have avoided him at any cost. Yet, the Lord chose him to bear His name before multitudes.

In fact in speaking of him the Lord said *'for he is a chosen vessel unto me, to bear my name before the Gentiles, and Kings, and the children of Israel: for I will show him how great things he must suffer for my name's sake'* (Acts 9:15–16).

There was not the slightest notion of glamour about such a call. It is good for us to see that. When we read Acts 8 and 9 we cannot help being convinced that this call came to Saul at a time when he was in his very prime in his religious status in the eyes of the world. Being well educated and influential, with the government's permission he wielded great authority over the Church. At the beginning of chapter 8 we see that he sanctioned Stephen's death by stoning.

Nobody can be proud of imperfection, but it is important to realize that God can, and does make something wonderful of imperfect sin-scarred human vessels like Saul, who later was given a new name, Paul. God is ever producing and establishing men and women, to honour His name in a world where people are still saying *'away with him, we will not have him to reign over us.'*

In the New Testament sense these are further examples of some of the types that God chooses for His mission. In Acts 13:2 we see how *'the Holy Ghost said, separate me Barnabas and Saul for the work whereunto I have called them.'* John 20:21 says *'As my Father hath sent me, even so send I you.'* That was Jesus' special commission to the men whom He had chosen to continue His work. In Gal. 1:15, *'But when it pleased God, who separated me from my mothers's womb, and called me by his grace, to reveal his Son in me, that I might preach him among the heathen . . .'* Also in Eph. 4:11 we read *'He gave some, apostles; and some, prophets; and some, evangelists; and some, pastors and teachers.'*

Each person in the above lists in the different passages had his special task to perform. Let us not forget that responsibility is deceitful and may easily rob us of much spiritual progress, but when commissioned as these early Christians were, the progress starts and finishes in God.

A little earlier we said that some people are drawn to mission. To clarify that point we must understand that in the Acts of the Apostles, Christians were not just carrying on from where the Old Testament people of God had left off. Those who were singled out for mission had Christ in their lives as Saviour. They were drawn to Him, the earliest ones by personal invitation which He had given them to follow Him. Later they were filled with the Holy Spirit at Pentecost. That was their only credential for mission. They were drawn, filled and commissioned. Through their ministry, Christianity today is spread all over the world. People everywhere have been and are being drawn to Christ by the activity of the Holy Spirit, and still many more are being filled and commissioned as witnesses to Christ. Being born to mission relates more to people of the Old Testament. Singled out, in the Scriptures, some appear to have little or no background, whilst others like Samson, or John the Baptist whom we have already considered, were born with their mission foretold; preordained. The fact remains, however, that our norm for comparison must always be the Christians who emerged from Acts 2. They continued steadfastly in the Apostles' doctrine and fellowship, and in breaking of bread, and in prayers. Herein was their strength.

It is interesting what the prophesy regarding the birth of John The Baptist says about wine and strong drink. He shall drink neither. It does not say that he 'must' not. It is understood that he shall not. The inference is clearly that instead *'he shall be filled with the Holy Spirit and power of Elias.'* It was as though the absence of alcohol in his drinking habits was equal but opposite to the strength of the mission that God had ordained for him. In other words drinking wine and strong drink was going to be incompatible with his mission. Why incompatible? I believe Leviticus 10:9, 10 answers the question.

This opens up a wide area of thought, as to why so many missions today have either collapsed, are moribund, or have ceased to be. In a little while we shall see what the Apostle Paul has to say about this, but first let us consult Joel. Chapter 1 is dedicated to denouncing liquor drinking for anyone who is engaged in mission. He appears to be particularly concerned for God's front men, men who stand out in ministry as leaders.

In Joel 1:5 he pleads urgently *'awake, ye drunk-ards, and weep; and howl, all ye drinkers of wine, because of the new wine; for it is cut off from your mouth.'* This is quite serious, the new wine being cut off from God's people. It is tantamount to saying that the Holy Spirit is separated from them. What a sad and gloomy picture. Joel illustrates the great disaster that is overtaking the Church, a contrary influence that robs many of God's people of their spiritual heritage. Obviously the old wine and the new do not mix, and we know that the new is better. If ever there is a book for the present day it is Joel. It cites the enemy barking God's fig tree clean bare (verse 7). Verse 9 says *'the meat offering and drink offering is cut off from the house of the Lord; the priests, the Lord's ministers, mourn:'* a catalogue of disaster, all because of the old wine. And we must remember this does not concern the Church only. When the Church is in decline the nation is never prosperous. *'Righteousness exalteth a nation: but sin is a reproach to any people'* says Prov. 14:34.

Joel sees the need for a getting together of all ministers. He urges a *'solemn assembly'* and a cry unto the Lord. He takes account of the fact that *'joy is withered away from the sons of men.'* Is this not true? Where are there happy people today? Our land has hardly ever been more lacking in joy.

Joel also considers our farmers and the crops which they produce. He considers even the beasts. *'How do the beasts groan! The herds of cattle are perplexed, because they have no pasture.'* What is that if it is not our modern B.S.E., Bovine spongiform encephalitis – 'mad cow disease?' So even the cattle are confused according to this, no doubt wondering why they have no pasture, and have to be fed on the same food as carnivorous animals whilst cooped up in restricted pens. Therefore, says Joel 1:20 *'the beasts of the field cry also unto thee.'*

This has to be a desperate state of affairs when even the animals are recognising that there is something wrong. Sadly, they appear to be ahead of many of us in their cry *'For we know that the whole creation groaneth and travaileth in pain together until now,'* says Paul in Rom. 8:22. He also supports Joel's concern regarding wine drinking by warning us, *'Be not drunk with wine, wherein is excess, but be filled with the Spirit.'* He was saying in other words, 'You can have as much of the Holy Spirit as you like. Be filled indeed with Him, but certainly not with wine for it will surely bring you into error, unlike the Holy Spirit who can only bring you into blessing. Remember that Jesus Christ (Rev. 1:6) has made us Kings and priests unto God and His Father. Consequently, drinks of this kind are not for Kings and priests of your particular lineage, leave such things to those who are ready to perish; those of the world who have 'heavy hearts.'

It could well be that Paul had in mind Prov. 31:4–7. *'It is not for Kings to drink wine; nor princes strong drink: lest they drink, and forget the law, and pervert the judgement of any of the afflicted. Give strong drink unto him that is ready to perish, and wine unto those that be of heavy hearts. Let him drink, and forget his poverty, and remember his misery no more.'*

41

Chapter 4

Power or No Power

We cannot over-emphasise that there is a lack of power in the Church today compared with that first flush of Holy Spirit activity amongst the Early Christians. But we must not settle for that. Scripture does not teach that in time the power could lessen. On the contrary, it is available – always available!

The problem is that over the years, slowly but surely we have suffered a spiritual erosion occasioned in our warfare. Paul was careful to warn the Corinthians of the possibility of this happening in the Church, and he told them what to do to counteract it in order to maintain what they had received from on High. He was concerned that in any event they should be sustained in spiritual buoyancy. I believe the same warning applies to us at the present time.

Paul said, *'For the weapons of "our" warfare are not carnal, but mighty through God to the pulling down of strong holds . . .'* (2 Cor. 10:4). That 'our' is really significant. The warfare is ours. We need to understand that.

There is a continual battle going on inside us, and but for the grace of God we could not stand. We are so often bombarded with doubts and fears, not to mention unbelief. These are enemies of the deepest dye, most destructive to faith and power. They were the very enemies that caused the children of Israel to die in their thousands in the wilderness, as God's wrath was poured out on them. God swore in His wrath that they would not enter His rest and according to Hebrews 4 we are warned not to fall into the same trap, as they did.

Looking back at what Paul says in 2 Cor. 10:5, we possess the weapons to be *'casting down imaginations, and every high thing that exalteth itself against the knowledge of God, and bringing into captivity every thought to the obedience of Christ.'* God grant that we really appreciate the importance of this.

Our minds can so easily become a breeding ground for vain imaginations. For example, how easy it is to imagine that the Holy Ghost power was only given by God to, as it were, launch the Church at Pentecost. How easy it is to think that that power is not available in the Church nowadays for healing the sick and even less so for raising the dead.

Most of us tend to be so unspiritual in our thinking that we are unable to embrace the supernatural and as a consequence reduce God to our own level of thinking. Vain imaginations- that is what those are. But the Bible says *'God is not a man, that he should lie; neither the son of man, that he should repent.'* Therefore we are encouraged to disallow these vain thoughts. We must not be found reducing God in our minds to a mere human god. Otherwise that way of thinking is as our text says *'every high thing that exalteth itself against the knowledge of God.'* It is like saying that we know more than He does. Quite unconsciously then we could be doing that at our peril, in the sense that through ignorance we are denying ourselves of God's best.

So these subtle enemies that operate largely in our thought process must all be brought into captivity to the obedience of Christ. They are dangerous.

In Joel 1:6-7 we have the perfect description of their character '. . . *strong, and without number, whose teeth are the teeth of a lion, and he hath the cheek teeth of a great lion. He hath laid my vine waste, and barked my fig tree: he hath made it clean bare . . .*' That is the picture of the Church without power. The power has been eroded, but how gradually that must have taken place.

One of the main troubles is that often we have the tendency to put our trust in experience. Yet, in our contention for the truth we must concede that experience is fallible, and the more we trust in it instead of in God's Word, the less we shall have of His promises being fulfilled in our lives. '*Let God be true and every man a liar.*'

Jesus in saying '*ye shall receive power "after" that the Holy Ghost is come upon you*' presupposes that that power is always available once you are baptized in the Holy Spirit. That is the significance, that afterwards you can be being perpetually replenished. One must admit that in some circles there is much talk of power, but when it comes down to the expression of it there is little or none. Let us take another look at what the Bible tells us of Jesus' life. He was anointed with the Holy Ghost and with 'power' and it is no secret as to what His lifestyle was afterwards. The power in His everyday walk was what singled Him out as different from everyone else. He did things that other people were unable to do. The most amazing thing was that He confessed He could do nothing of Himself, and yet He did everything. The power that was upon His life benefited all who sought after Him for whatever reasons.

I went to a church the other day where the visiting preacher was an eminent evangelist whose ministry was particularly to Asia. The church was packed and the air of expectancy was heightened as the congregation sang, shouted, clapped, danced and shrieked to the uplifting strains of the flute, violin, guitar, drums and piano led by a local vocalist, displaying his confidence in Christ.

I must add, the video camera was poised to capture every moment of that power extravaganza.

The preamble now over, the Pastor invited the celebrated evangelist to the platform, a well dressed middle aged man of modest height. In his handsomely tailored suit, his slightly receding hair line and dark complexion seemed to give him extra poise for the occasion. Hardly taking a breath he began to speak, announcing as he did that the power of God was present. It was there he emphasised, 'to heal the sick (and there were many) to drive out the Devil, and to give liberty for praising the Lord.'

That, as far as I was concerned, was a most encouraging opening and I couldn't help thinking that here was a man after my own heart. He was going to demonstrate the power of God; we were going to be really blessed.

As it turned out the evangelist spoke very interestingly, maintaining a flow of words that few could match. Sadly, however, right up to the conclusion there was no evidence that anyone had received healing, the baptism in the Holy Spirit or any of the things that were promised.

You can imagine how disappointed I was, and no doubt many others were also. Nevertheless, one ought not to criticise, but would do well to pray for such a preacher. The feeling is that he may seek and receive such an anointing from God that will enable him whenever he preaches to demonstrate the power of God. According to the Scriptures signs should follow such a ministry *'The Kingdom of God is not in word,'* said Paul, *'but in power'* (1 Cor. 4:20). In writing to the Corinthians he assured them of his own frailties, but was at pains to explain that such did not hinder God's power being manifest in his ministry. *'I was with you in weakness, in fear and in much trembling'* Paul said. *'And my speech and my preaching'* he continued *'was not with enticing words of man's wisdom, but in demonstration of the Spirit and of power; that your faith should not stand in the wisdom of men, but in the power of God'* (1 Cor. 2:3–5).

The Enemy Lost The Battle

A year or two ago I was asked to address a certain Christian group meeting in a house about a mile or so from my home. On arrival there to my astonishment the house was full of people all apparently seeking

God. But there was a note of sadness. The sister in Christ who had invited me soon informed me that her daughter (whom we might call Helen) was anorexic. As far as the family were concerned her life was in jeopardy; the worst was imminent.

Of course, such information was not designed to inspire confidence. But I remembered the words of Jesus *'Lo, I am with you alway'* (Matt. 28:20). Taking that to mean He is with me in all circumstances, in all places and at all times, I regained my composure, greeted the company of people, chose the place in which I should stand, and began to speak.

I cannot now recall the precise text from which I spoke, but my entire emphasis was on exalting Jesus. We were gathered in the largest room in the house, one especially arranged for the meeting. All the seats were taken, as I stood with my Bible in my hand. When I had spoken for about fifteen minutes a door on my left swung open and in walked a shadowy young lady of about five feet seven inches tall, very pale and slight of body, little more than a skeleton. She made her way over to my right side and sat on the floor no more than three feet from me. That was Helen.

I paused only for a moment for a silent acknowledgement of our last entrant and proceeded to exalt the Saviour. After a few more minutes Helen left the room through the door by which she had entered.

Soon after that, her mother also left by the same door. I didn't expect their departure to make any difference to the afternoon's proceedings, but hardly had I finished my talk when I heard a tremendous uproar above our heads. To this day I am not sure that everybody in that house heard what I heard. It was like a deafening trundle of one thousand steam locomotives making their way through the rooms upstairs. It was horrendous. But even then I could hear the voice of Helen's mother, 'Come, Brother McCatty, come quickly. The Devil has got Helen. Come!'

I had the presence of mind not to hurry despite the urgent plea, thinking 'If it is really the Devil it takes the Lord to deliver her and He is already in control.' I therefore turned round and was composedly going to the door when the mother rushed in and grabbed my hand, escorting me to the uppermost room in the house.

The noise had by this time subsided as we climbed the three flights of stairs. My heart was pounding. I knew I could not turn back, but had to face up to whatever the challenge was. Then Helen's mother said 'That's the room. The Devil has got her in there.' She pointed to a door behind which the noise that I had heard earlier downstairs was beginning again. The only difference was that this time it was in short bursts.

We stood looking at the door and slowly got closer and closer to it. My hostess was on my right side and affectionately put her left arm around my waist, as though helping me forward. It was my own idea that we should enter the room together. I didn't realize that she had something different in mind, and soon discovered the true reason why her arm was around my waist. With her left hand she caught hold of the door handle, and with the other, as already described, she gently manoeuvred me as though we were really together, opened the door, pushed me inside the room and retreated, shutting the door behind her.

I don't know how my heart stayed in its place, but I am sure of one thing. I must have felt like Daniel in the 'den of lions' (Dan, 6:16). Looking across the room I felt there was no strength in me to move an inch. There on a bed on her hands and knees was Helen facing me squarely. Her eyes filled with terror as she glowered and roared at me like a lioness. Her curly, black, shoulder length hair was rising and falling, as one would expect it to be in the wind. From that crouched position she raised her right hand and pointing at me menacingly, yelled, 'Put that light out. Put that light out. I will . . .'

Of course, as far as I was concerned there was no light to put out, and I could not obey her orders in any event. Rather, taking my counsel from the Holy Spirit I raised my hand quickly and pointing directly at her I shouted, 'I smite you in the name of Jesus.'

She instantly fell flat on the bed as dead, whereupon I breathed a sigh of relief. Taking no chances I waited a minute or two just to make sure that the enemy was truly smitten, before I went up to Helen. When I felt satisfied that all was well, there being no further evidence of terror in the room, I went up to the bed and called out, 'Helen, how are you?' She was at this time thoroughly motionless, but opening her eyes she responded to my inquiry with the words 'Praise the Lord! I am well, thank you. Jesus is wonderful!'

Her voice was now mellow, the tone was inviting, reassuring and pleasant. The Lord had delivered Helen and in a short while she was downstairs restored to her family, the Fellowship and society. *'Call upon me in the day of trouble: I will deliver thee, and thou shalt glorify me'* says Psalm 50:15.

The question which this chapter ask is: Do we want power in our Christian walk, or are we content to settle for the mediocre – just words and meaningless ritual? There are millions of people just like Helen. Some of them are living just a stone's throw from where you are right now. They are bound up with every horrible torture Satan can conceive to throw at them. They need answers – and they need someone with God's power flowing into their lives to bring them those answers.

The drug addict, the alcoholic, the lonely single mother struggling to bring up her child, they all need you and me to reach out to them with His love, and with the Holy Ghost power He has made available to us.

Chapter 5

Give God a Chance – Go Ye!

To be effective we cannot pray apologetically. Neither can we praise or worship God with a cold heart. They that worship Him must do so *'in Spirit and in Truth.'* As we have already seen, Paul in writing to the Ephesians exhorted them *'to be filled with the Spirit'* (Eph. 5:18). Paul knew from personal experience that that filling was the key to a triumphant life in Christ, through the warmth of the Spirit.

When Jesus said *'Go ye therefore, and teach all nations,'* there were no ifs or buts, as to the success that would follow. Power from on High was going to be granted by the Father to the apostles, and those who received salvation through their ministry, to effect Jesus' command.

It is interesting to note the number of times the word 'full', or 'filled', appears in the Acts of the Apostles regarding the Christian life (Acts 2:4; 4:8,31; 6:8; 11:24). Whatever our views might be on this subject, the challenge remains as to whether we have received fullness. It is sobering to realise what power, zeal, authority, love and diligence we forfeit when the Spirit is ignored. In such circumstances it might well be said that we have settled for a *'well of water'* John 4:14, instead of the *'rivers of living water,'* John 7:38. Thinking of this, one is also reminded of the prophet David's statement in his passion for Christ, *'Thy people shall be willing in the day of thy power, in the beauties of holiness from the womb of the morning: thou hast the dew of thy youth . . .'* (Psa. 110:3).

It is marvellous that David by the Spirit of the Lord looked down the corridors of time to the present day, signifying in no uncertain way the day of the Spirit, the day of the Lord's power. He recognised the Church of Christ, as though it were ablaze with the Holy Spirit's power, focusing on Christ as Lord, the One and only Object of all praise, honour and adoration. David forsaw modern Christians filled with the Spirit of God willingly worshipping the Lord in the Beauty of His personal Holiness. Let us recall *'the children of Ephraim'* although *'being armed, and carrying bows, turned back in the day of battle'* (Psa. 78:9). We can hardly say that they were willing at that most critical time to do God's will. No doubt David might have been thinking of them when he gave that prophecy. As we shall see, they were equipped for battle, but they did not have the will to fight. Their being armed suggests that they had the Word of God, which Paul tells us in Eph 6 is the *'sword of the Spirit.'* They were even carrying bows, meaning they had ammunition and had gone so far toward the battle yet they could not engage the Enemy, but retreated. They were like a beautiful motor car that has a powerful engine and all the capacity for

52

speed and for giving pleasure to its owner but there is no fuel in it. How dishonourable! How deflating for any nation to have trained soldiers who are like that, who in times of conflict refuse to advance.

In the spiritual sense the missing ingredient (the fuel) was the Holy Spirit. He makes people willing! He gives us the Divine impetus to willingly go forward in the day of battle, the day of the Lord's power. We are certainly not destined to retreat. *'We are more than conquerors through Him that loved us.'* His Spirit being with us, we have the ability not only to enjoy our personal freedom but to liberate those who are helplessly held in captivity.

Other circumstances which might have concerned David in his passion could have been the twelve spies who went to investigate the land of Caanan. All but two came back with a very negative report. They said it was a good land possessing all the desirable things just as God had said, 'but', there were giants there, formidable giants. They reported convincingly that in no way should Israel consider entry, for when they had visited they were like grasshoppers compared with the inhabitants. The two who came back with encouraging words were Joshua and Caleb. They didn't say the giants were not there. They didn't say they were not colossal and dreadful looking. What Caleb said was this: *'Let us go up at once, and possess it; for we are well able to overcome it.'* (Num. 13:30).

That was not a natural statement, but spiritual. What the others said was natural. They spoke naturally, because they thought that way, not being motivated by the Spirit of the Lord. There was going to be a penalty for that, but a wonderful accolade and eternal blessing for both Caleb and Joshua.

Verses 23,24 of Numbers 14 says, *'surely they shall not see the land which I sware unto their fathers, neither shall any of them that provoked me see it: but my servant Caleb, because he had another Spirit with him, and hath followed me fully, him will I bring into the land whereinto he went; and his seed shall possess it.'* Virtually the same is repeated later in the chapter, that they shall not enter the land *'save Caleb the son of Jephunneh, and Joshua the son of Nun.'* Not only were those willing, but they had faith that no one else seemed to have in the promise of God to Israel.

In Matthew 18:18, Jesus says, *'Verily I say unto you, whatsoever ye shall bind on earth shall be bound in heaven: and whatsoever ye shall loose on earth shall be loosed in heaven.'* On the spiritual battlefield this is not just encouraging, it is vital to our being successful, remembering always that the battle is not ours, it is the Lord's. In His name we have power to bind or set free.

As we have said earlier, this is the day of His power. We do not necessarily have to make a conscious effort to obey His rules or commands; the Holy Spirit sees to those details. His practical support is always at hand, providing in the New Testament sense we are filled with the Spirit.

Consider what Jesus says to Philadelphia *'thou hast a little strength'* (Rev. 3:8). That is not a rebuke. On the contrary it is warm encouragement implying

54

that He is with them. He will give all the support needed. That 'all power', which is given unto Him both in heaven and in earth will always operate on our behalf. Would it not be wonderful if we were conscious of His faith being available to us at all times? It is a great blessing to read of the stance that Paul the Apostle maintained in front of Nero, *'No man stood with me'* (2 Tim. 4:16). In one sense, was that not disappointing, revealing as it does that we cannot depend on any human being, at least not wholly? In a real crisis there can be only one infallible support, the Lord.

So Paul ends his statement with prayer for those who had failed him, *'That it may not be laid to their charge.'* And it is not surprising to find him saying later, *'Notwithstanding the Lord stood with me, and strengthened me . . . and I was delivered out of the mouth of the lion.'* Your lion could be poised to pounce on you right now. Will he succeed?

To be filled with the Spirit then is to be filled with God, a revolutionary mighty experience that warms up the coldest heart. That is why we read in the Acts, of folk being aglow with the Spirit. Every aspect of their being became responsive to God. The supernatural was abundantly manifested in them, as individuals and in their church meetings. There were people being saved (born again), healings were taking place, devils were being cast out and there were many blessings of judgement, miracles and other supernatural happenings amongst them. At one of their earliest preachings three thousand surrendered to Christ, and shortly afterwards five thousand did the same. There was a great spiritual awakening. We belong to a supernatural body after all, the Body of Christ, and it is God's will to move in and through us supernaturally. *'For it is God which worketh in you both to will and to do of His good pleasure'* (Phil. 2:13).

After That Upper Room Experience

In the Acts we are constantly faced with this fact. We see throughout the whole book the tremendous movings of God through His people, as they, under the direct auspices of the Holy Spirit, called upon Him. In chapter 1, when the Lord Jesus ascended, angelic beings appeared. That was obviously not a natural phenomenon.

In chapter 2, there were tongues of fire accompanied by a mighty rushing wind bursting in upon those who patiently waited in that upper room for the coming of the Holy Ghost. What an experience that was! The first of its kind ever to take place in the earth. The Christian Church was launched, as it were in an unparalleled blaze of glory. Weak men, cowardly men, fearful men, the ignorant and unlearned, all received from the hand of the Father the mighty outpouring of the Holy Ghost. What transforming power that was!

They left that upper room lion-hearted, bold, full of confidence in proclaiming that Jesus was Christ. That was the main fact in the change that the disciples underwent. All without equivocation boldly and openly confessed Jesus Christ as Saviour, Lord, Healer and Baptizer in the Holy Spirit.

Reviewing their Acts, here is a synopsis of the catalogue of events. We shall devote a little space to at least one or two of the incidents in the chapters. In chapter 3, a lame man was miraculously made whole. He had been unwell from birth and used to be put down at the church gate where he begged from the people who passed by. When he saw Peter and John passing he asked them for some money. *'And Peter, fastening his eyes upon him with John said "Look on us."'* Isn't it interesting that he didn't say look to Jesus, but rather "look on us". They knew that they had received power from high to help that man, and anyone else who would be helped.

No doubt by the resident power of the Holy Spirit the apostles could recall that Jesus had told them *'Occupy till I come.'* In other words, 'take my place until I return'. Therefore, Peter further said to the lame man *'Silver and gold have I none; but such as I have give I thee: in the name of Jesus Christ of Nazareth rise up and walk.'*

Did that man hesitate to obey? Did he say, 'well, I am not used to walking, I don't think I'll be able to manage it?' Peter simply *'Took him by the right hand, and lifted him up: and immediately his feet and ankle bones received strength. And he leaping up; stood, and walked and entered with them into the temple, walking, and leaping and praising God.'* Wasn't that tremendous! He wasn't praising Peter or John, but God. That just goes to show that the Holy Spirit is not with us to glorify us, but the One who sent Him. Jesus said this: *'He shall glorify me: for he shall receive of mine, and shall shew it unto you.'* (John 16:14)

There is something else well worth noting about this incident. That man who had been lame, instantly went to church. He was also so excited at what God had done for him that he was not only walking, but leaping and praising God in church.

Can you see him doing that in some of our modern day sophisticated churches where dignity, and order according to religion, is paramount? And just imagine him shouting out, 'Praise the Lord!' Not once or twice, but several times with as much gusto as he could muster? What would his plight be? The Holy Spirit, however, gives such freedom to people who are touched by Him. The Bible speaks of *the liberty of the sons of God,* and there is another text that says *Where the Spirit of the Lord is, there is liberty.* Paul had to rebuke a certain group of Spirit-filled Christians because they were excessive in their display of spiritual exuberance. Perhaps they were extremely fanatical. This is possibly something that most people whose lives have been touched by the Lord in this special way need to watch. We can be aglow with the Spirit and indeed should be, but we can certainly do without fanaticism and foolishness. The freedom of the Spirit doesn't make us into oddities.

There is consummate dignity about the Spirit-filled man or woman whose lifestyle is under the constraint and restraint of the Word of God. In these days emotion is not frowned upon or rejected as much as it was a few years ago. We have to thank God for that, for He is the Creator of our emotions after all, and we need to praise Him with all our being. Yet, there is need for balance in all things.

Possessing the liberty of the Spirit does not mean that we have to behave like clowns, and make our meetings or churches look like circuses or fairs, – that becomes ridiculous to an already critical world. Paul's warning to the Spirit-filled was this: *'Let all things be done decently and in order.'*

Allowances can be made for the new convert or the newly baptized in the Holy Spirit, but there can be no pardon for people who have walked with the Lord for a long time who persistently act in such a way that the unsaved/unregenerate sees them as insane. Psalm 100 says *'Serve the Lord with gladness,'* not madness.

Acts 4 recounts the visitation of the Holy Spirit after an incident with certain rulers involving Peter and John. The rulers were *'grieved that they taught the people, and preached through Jesus the resurrection from the dead.'* Therefore they had them arrested and put in gaol, but that was only after about 5,000 men had received Christ as Saviour. That was a good record.

Doesn't that make some of our preaching sound hollow? Here were a couple of men whom the people in another place had dubbed unlearned and ignorant, for so they did appear, but they simply preached Christ, and all that number of souls were gathered into the Kingdom.

Obedience To The Call Is An Imperative
The backlash did not seem to deter Peter and John.

After spending the night in prison they were brought out before the judges to be questioned. The main thing that seemed to bother the judges was that they could not understand how these men had such phenomenal influence over the people and over their circumstances. They questioned them in particular regarding the man they had healed. *'By what power, or by what name, have ye done this?'* they inquired.

The answer was ready to hand. Peter, filled with the Holy Ghost unashamedly told them *'That by the name of Jesus Christ of Nazareth, whom ye crucified, whom God raised from the dead, even by Him doth this man stand here before you whole.'* There was no backing down, no nuance of excuse or apology, no expression of cleverness; only God-given commonsense and Holy Ghost boldness was Peter's defence.

How this man's testimony must have gladdened the heart of God! The Bible says *'When they saw the boldness of Peter and John, and perceived that they were unlearned and ignorant men, they marvelled; and they took knowledge of them that they had been with Jesus.'*

Yes, they had been with Him- walking the dusty roads. They had been with the giver of Life, as the Teacher, the Healer, the Great Physician, the One who raised Lazarus from the dead, gave sight to the blind, and speech to the dumb. They had also been with Him when He had received ridicule and mocking, without retort. On the other hand they had been with Him when He received many an accolade without self-gratification, as the Holy

Spirit guided and directed Him; and now they were doing even as He had done, and going through many experiences similar to those through which He had gone. Their accusers could find no fault in them, but in order to justify themselves they not only threatened, but *'commanded them not to speak at all nor teach in the name of Jesus.'*

There was no way that Peter and John could have obeyed that directive. They were already under heaven's command. Hence their testimony was to the effect that God is to be obeyed rather than men *'For we cannot but speak the things which we have seen and heard.'*

This their testimony was dynamic and could not be ignored. Therefore the judges freed them, but as we might expect, the apostles still could not keep silence, nor refrain from using the name of Jesus. In a little while they were to be found publicly presenting their petitions to God in that same name, not only that they might be bold, but that healing might be a part of their ministry in the name of Jesus. God immediately showed His approval of them: *'For when they prayed, the place was shaken where they were assembled together; and they were all filled with the Holy Ghost, and they spake the Word of God with boldness.'*

Peter and John, along with many other great heroes of Scripture, did one thing which distinguished them from so many who have made up the Body of Christ down through the centuries. They went! They simply rose up in obedience to the call of God and trusted Him to equip them for the tasks He was to give them. Many Christians will never venture beyond the front door of their church. They see Christianity as a sort of 'service industry' of which they are the prime benificiaries.

But God intended more than that we sit back in our comfortable pews and be pampered by 'good' sermons and pretty singing. He wants us out where the need is, displaying lives filled with His compassion, lives filled with His power.

Can God use us in the same way as He used Peter and John? Unless we put ourselves in that position – unless we give God a chance – who can tell what He wants to do in our lives? Unless we go, how can we know?

Chapter 6

Praying Down the Fire

We have already learned much from our look at the life of Elijah. He was truly a man willing to give God a chance. There can be no more dramatic demonstration of that fact than Elijah's encounter with the prophets of Baal.

As requested by Elijah all Israel were duly gathered together. There were the eight hundred and fifty (false) prophets included, and the scene was set for a contest, which was designed for all to prove conclusively who was the right God to worship. Just before it began we see Elijah (1 Kings 18:22) bemoaning the fact that he was standing alone. He said *'I, even I only, remain a prophet of the Lord; but Baal's prophets are four hundred and fifty men.'*

This could appear strange or even unrealistic that God's man of faith and power had suddenly become weak-kneed, but was he really? I believe it was in the wisdom of God that he spoke like that. It was not a negative or weak confession, but a powerful part of his stratagem. One aspect of what it did was to emphasise the fact that there was, as it were, a built-in bias in the contest in favour of those prophets, and indeed all Israel. Therefore when the results of the contest were examined it could never at any time be said that Elijah cheated.

He told them that there should be two bullocks for the sacrifice. They should choose one *'for themselves, and cut it in pieces, and lay it on wood, and put no fire under'* it. They should call on the name of their gods for fire to consume their sacrifice, but when it was his turn he would *'call on the name of the Lord: and the God that answereth by fire, let him be God.'*

The people all agreed that this was the correct basis for a fair contest, whereupon Elijah said something like this to the prophets of Baal. 'As there are so many of you, sacrifice your bullock first. I can wait, you take as much time as you find necessary!' And they did, calling in vain on Baal practically all day. The Bible says *'there was no voice, nor any that answered.'* Does this not illustrate the lengths to which some people will go in vain attempts at finding the solution to their needs, when the real answer is only a prayer away? *'They prophesied until the time of the offering of the evening sacrifice, that there was neither voice, nor any to answer, nor any that regarded.'*

There was nothing more that they could have done. They had even *'leaped upon the altar.'* They had cried aloud and drawn their own blood, by cutting themselves with knives and lancets, but their god (Baal) remained silent. What was the good of their prophecy? As we have already seen, the only prophecy that has any value is that which is from the Lord.

As they persisted in their folly, Elijah seized upon

the opportunity to introduce a little comic relief into the situation. Mighty man of God that he was, you would hardly think that he had any time for a joke, but he could see the funny side of things. *'Cry aloud,'* he said, *'for he is a god; either he is talking, or he is pursuing, or he is in a journey, or peradventure he sleepeth and must be awaked,'* but still there was no change.

'And Elijah said unto all the people, Come near unto me. And all the people came near unto him' (1 Kings 18:30). Obviously he was not going to do anything behind their backs and this had to be plainly seen, to avoid suspicion. So what was the first thing he did? He did not say, 'you are all wrong and I am right. Your god isn't any good.'

He did not inquire into the social services. He did not apply any of the then rules of politics, which might well have been a system of taking away some of this world's goods, from those who have most to give to those who have least. He did not try to create new ministries for running this or that government department which had failed. Nor did he counsel with the state ecologists, scientists, the Met Office or whatever. Recall that the country as a viable autonomous state had reached its nadir. Would Elijah have to say it is too far gone?

No! *'He repaired the altar of the Lord that was broken down.'* Does this not awaken within us a desire to see the same happening in our nation, the altar of the Lord being repaired? Acknowledging the state of things everywhere around us, in the light of God's Word, spiritually and morally the altar of the Lord is indeed broken down. Jesus helps in Matthew 23:19–22 in understanding this altar. He explains that it is equal to the offerings which are placed upon it. The spiritual significance is that Christ is both Altar and Sacrifice. It is important for us to lay hold of this.

As the Sacrificial Lamb of God, Christ possesses in Himself the ability to sustain this dual role. He is great enough for anything. The sweet odour that rises from the burning of the Sacrifice on that precious Altar is exquisitely pleasing to God the Father, thus enabling Him to bless rather than to curse men.

This latter was exactly what Elijah had in mind. In order to reverse the curse that overshadowed Samaria under idolatry he would first have this precious odour going up to God. The lesson we learn from the Scriptures regarding this is that such a fragrance could only be achieved by sacrifice. There were indeed other offerings placed on the altar, as well as 'burnt offerings,' but on every occasion it is like the burning of incense whereby a sweet fragrance (typifying Christ) would rise to God, enabling Him to act in infinite grace and mercy toward mankind (ref: Exodus 30:27,28. Leviticus 6:9). So we now know that an altar is a place of sacrifice where we part with things. We sacrifice them to God. Spiritually speaking, it is that place where we hand over to God, firstly our lives, then our time, money, pride, affections . . . the list is endless. But when God has our lives in His care that list is His responsibility. By His Spirit He leads us *'in the paths of righteousness for His name's sake.'* In other words He leads us in such a way that we have right standing with Him, and that is all that matters. Therefore, that was what Elijah did in the presence of all the people whom he had asked to draw near to him. He prayed, he communed with God. He worshipped Him, and making no secret of it, he laid the foundation not only for God's presence, but for His blessings to flow.

Elijah taught those needy people the only right way of living. Exodus 20:24,25 helps to explain this. *'An altar of earth thou shalt make unto me, and shalt sacrifice thereon thy burnt offerings, and thy peace offerings . . . I will come unto thee, and I will bless thee.'* His coming is of the greatest importance, and if the 'altar' of the Lord is not present neither is His blessing. *'The blessing of the Lord,'* says Proverbs 10:22, *'it maketh rich, and He addeth no sorrow with it.'* Were the people of Israel under Ahab with those false prophets lacking in blessing? Were they lacking in riches? Were they sorrowful?

There was now a sound foundation upon which Elijah could build. The Lord's altar was there in a good state of repair. So *'Elijah took twelve stones, according to the number of the tribes of the sons of Jacob, unto whom the word of the Lord came, saying, Israel shall be thy name: and with the stones he built an altar in the name of the Lord: and he made a trench about the altar, as great as would contain two measures of seed.'*

There was already a functional altar of the Lord, why then was Elijah erecting another? That is a vital question. Both are equally important in their own setting. The first signifying worship, and the second, sacrifice. Only a man of God of Elijah's calibre would have perceived that. It is little wonder that his prayers were effectual and fervent.

So he built this altar himself as a spiritually intelligent person bearing in mind the very covenant of God with his predecessor Jacob: *'I am the Lord God of Abraham thy father, and the God of Isaac: the land whereon thou liest, to thee will I give it, and to thy seed; and thy seed shall be as the dust of the earth . . . and in thy seed shall all the families of the earth be blessed'* (Gen. 28:13,14).

When The Fire Fell

Elijah knew that he could hold God to His own Word, and the altar that he was making in His name was a robust reminder of that fact. His blessing would fall on Israel. Hardly had he finished the building with the trench around it than he cut the bullock in pieces, and laid him on the wood, and said *'Fill four barrels with water, and pour it on the sacrifice, and on the wood.'* I can imagine the onlookers saying he was crazy. Eight hundred and fifty prophets failed to have their sacrifice ignite and it was dry. What chance did Elijah have of fire coming upon an altar like that, so sodden with water!

What I would like to know is this: From where did Elijah manage to get water after all? There was none in all the land at that time after years of drought. That was a miracle! He had the folk pouring water on as though there was a regular supply – one, two, three barrels full: '*And the water ran round about the altar; and he filled the trench also with water.*' That was wonderful: the water symbolising the Holy Spirit. Though there was an unquestionable dearth of Holy Spirit power throughout Israel, here was one man demonstrating that he had suffered no shortage at all, and was thoroughly in unison with God.

The hour of reckoning had fully arrived and all had waited with bated breath, as Elijah began to pray. How effective would this prayer be? It is interesting that he called upon the '*Lord God of Abraham, Isaac, and of Israel.*'

As this was a public prayer uttered amongst people who were used to worshipping other gods, it was necessary we might think for him to specify that the One upon whom he was now calling, was the same as his famous forefathers had worshipped. On the other hand, it might have been his way of reminding God that he had respect for His faithfulness to those saintly men of old, and was trusting Him for the same treatment. Either was justified anyhow, and even in my own private prayers sometimes I find myself talking with God like that; recalling the names of men and women of high spiritual integrity who manifestly had favour with God. What matters most, however, is the result. The next part of Elijah's prayer was an emphatic plea that God should let it be known that He was God in Israel, and that he was His servant working under His instruction.

Earlier, we did say that in prayers which are led by the Holy Spirit the specific words are not the most important consideration, but the attitude is. Prayers that are going to be answered begin in the very heart of God, the guarantee of effectiveness. With Elijah, the attitude was that God should be seen and acknowledged for who He really is: in the words of Scripture *'That this people may know that thou art the Lord God, and that thou hast turned their heart back again'* (1 Kings 18:37).

The fire did indeed fall, consuming not only the wood and the meat (the bullock) but, *'the stones, and the dust, and licked up the water that was in the trench.'* There was therefore no room for doubt as to who was the right God to worship. When all the people saw what had happened, *'They fell on their faces: and they said, The LORD, He is the God; the LORD, He is the God.'*

It was a wonderful victory for Elijah, a tremendous salvation and blessing for the people, and as for God He was truly vindicated, but that is not the end of the story. The land had to be purged of its corruptors, the false prophets. Elijah issued the command that they should all be arrested. *'Let not one of them escape,'* he said. In other words idolatry (rebellion against God) and the very perpetrators of such must be thoroughly expunged, before God's blessing could come upon the land.

Therefore, taking the initiative, *'Elijah brought them* (the false prophets) *down to the brook Kishon, and slew them there.'*

That might seem a hard thing, even merciless. Yet, we must remember that, *'The wages of sin is death.'* The Bible makes that quite clear. Well, those prophets received their earnings at the hands of the man whom God had appointed paymaster. We can thank God that we are living in a different time, the day of grace according to the Scriptures. Grace was not available then, but now Jesus has come with Good News to modern man. *'For the law was given by Moses, but grace and truth came by Jesus Christ'* (John 1:17). The wages of sin is still death. That has not changed, *'But the gift of God is eternal life through Jesus Christ our Lord.'* For nearly two thousand years this has been the Good News that sinners, idolators, rebels, liars, thieves, rapists, God-haters, agnostics, atheists, murderers, and everybody else can individually or collectively turn to God in repentance, and receive instant forgiveness and cleansing. It is marvellous! Altogether precious! We cannot merit this, it is the free gift of God offered to all mankind, for on Calvary Jesus (the Sacrificial Lamb) has fully paid for our sin in His own body. He died, *'The Just for the unjust, to bring us to God.'*

It would have been an awful waste of life if the death of those prophets was the end of the story, but it was not. It was the prelude to a great national change, in respect of the utter bankruptcy, (spiritually as well as economically), decadence, and not to mention despondency and shame. It was the manifest overthrow of idolatry, and was the herald of the downpour of much blessing.

Elijah was excited for he knew what was about to happen. So he *'said unto Ahab, get thee up, eat and drink; for there is a sound of abundance of rain.'* Wasn't that amazing? After all that had recently taken place, for which Ahab the heathen King might well have been seething with hate and contempt for Elijah, he was able to speak to him as though they were friends. How true it is that *'When a man's ways please the LORD, He maketh even his enemies to be at peace with him'* (Pro. 16:7).

Ahab went and had his meal, as advised, in preparation for what was about to happen. At the same time Elijah took the opportunity to slip off to the top of the Mountain to have a few words with God. Throwing himself down onto the ground and putting *'his face between his knees,'* he refreshed himself in prayer and fellowship with the Almighty. We are unable to say exactly what Elijah's prayer was, as we are not told. What is clear though is that he got through. He had heard from God that rain was on its way. When one counsels with God in that way and receives an answer like that, there is no equivocation. Rousing himself, Elijah said to his servant, *'Go up now, look toward the sea'.* What for? the servant might have asked, but he did not. *'He went, and looked,'* as was requested, most likely not having a clue as to what he might expect. Promptly returning to his master he said, *'There is nothing.'* But Elijah insisted *'Go again seven times.'*

The young man obediently went a second time, only to find that there was still nothing to see. It wasn't until he had gone the seven times according to his master's command that he was able to report seeing something. Should this not be a signal lesson for us, at least as to perseverance? We must come back to this later, but for the moment let us consider what Elijah's servant saw. There was not much, only a little cloud arising *'out of the sea, like a man's hand.'*

Perceiving that God was in that report Elijah said, 'that is it, go quickly and tell Ahab to prepare his chariot for getting to Jezreel before the rain starts.' No sooner had Ahab got the message than he was on his way, *'And there was a great rain . . . And the hand of the Lord was on Elijah; and he girded up his loins, and ran before Ahab to the entrance of Jezreel'.*

There are tremendous lessons to be learned from the fact that Elijah's servant had to go and look seven times towards the sea before he saw anything. That was no coincidence. On the seventh day God rested from the work of Creation, and we know that seven speaks of completeness or fullness.

Therefore the seven times for us here would speak of patience backed by Divine revelation, the hallmark of what is meant by praying with confidence. Elijah persisted in sending his servant to look because he had counselled with God. In his spirit he already saw that cloud, and therefore knew that his servant was not on a fools errand.

This brings to mind Paul's teaching on perseverance (Eph.6:18) *'Praying always with all prayer and supplication in the Spirit, and watching thereunto with all perseverance and supplication for all saints . . .'* He does not speak of this as something natural, but spiritual. Perseverance, according to Paul, is a gift from God which we are expected to use; if we do not, then we might find ourselves quitting our position before Him over certain matters just when we might have got through to a satisfactory conclusion. How persistent was Elijah? How dedicated was he to what he perceived God was about to do?

If both Elijah and Paul were with us today they would point out that with God everything is timed. Timing is of the utmost importance to Him.

Consider these Scriptures for instance: *'For when we were without strength in due time Christ died for the ungodly'* (Rom. 5:6). *'And when the day of Pentecost was fully come, they were all with one accord in one place'* (Acts 2:1 . . .). *'Then Jesus said unto them, my time is not yet come'* (John 7:6). *'To everything there is a season, and a time to every purpose under the heaven'* (Ecc. 3:1). So Jesus warns us in Acts 1:7, *'It is not for you to know the times or the seasons, which the Father hath put in His own power.'* He gives us all the power that we need for everything that we have to do.

If we ever have to pray over any matter several times before receiving an answer, we do not have to quit praying, any more than Elijah's servant had to stop going to look out to sea for 'fully' seven times. Perseverance then, was the key to that situation, and it still is. *'Therefore, my beloved brethren, be ye stedfast, unmoveable, always abounding in the work of the Lord, forasmuch as ye know that your labour is not in vain in the Lord'* (1 Cor. 15:58).

Chapter 7

The Secret of Serving

We have already seen that the Early Church was endowed with people of tremendous spiritual vigour. The Acts of the Apostles record what happened to Paul, Peter and others, as they went about preaching the gospel and teaching the Word of God. An interesting exercise might be to forget for a moment everything we know about these men of God and to look at them with fresh eyes to see the impact they made on their times.

In prayer they were indomitable. In ministry they were effective. In courage and boldness they were irrepressible. Their prayers reached upward and evidenced a power we have seldom, if ever, seen. They knew that they only had to ask in Jesus' name for healing, deliverance from earthquakes, demons, evil spirits and even death, and their requests would be granted. They had the certainty of God's presence with them in every circumstance, supporting and directing their lives. So persuaded were they of these things that whatever happened either to them or in their ministry they could still praise God.

Remember Paul and Silas charged by the Romans of corruption? Brought before the magistrates they were convicted and sentenced. Their suffering was awful! They were stripped, beaten and cast into prison – all for healing a young woman who had followed them day by day, and was, as the Bible shows 'demon-possessed.'

Now they were put into chains in prison, battered and neglected, but certainly not dejected. For them, it was a fine opportunity to celebrate Jesus. Neither said to the other, 'Why has this happened to us?' as some of us might have done. Their backs were bleeding and sore from the beating. They were tired, unwashed and hungry, but not disconsolate, instead they prayed, sang hymns, and made melody unto the Lord.

Around midnight there was an earthquake. To the unsuspecting this would have been misery piled on misery, indeed one disaster after another. But not so for Paul and Silas. They were strong in the Lord and knew that He was in charge. As they continued rejoicing in Him their chains fell off, the doors were opened and instead of a disaster there was nothing but triumph. How this reminds us of what Jesus says in John 8:32: *'And ye shall know the truth, and the truth shall make you free.'* Those apostles were free, born free – born of God and under His mighty protection. The gaoler's chains could not hold them. He was so amazed at what had taken place that not only he, but his entire family were led to accept Jesus Christ as Saviour.

Tremendous! Jesus further says in the same chapter, verse 36: *'If the Son therefore shall make you free, ye shall be free indeed.'* No prison, no circumstance, can be strong enough to hold God's anointed captive. The apostles prevailed in prayer and so must we.

It is nothing short of a revelation to check and see how many people were healed of their diseases by the prayers of those mighty men of God. Reflect on how those men of faith arrived at such an impregnable stance in God. From where had they found this unshakeable assurance, power and joy that carried them through all their adversities and all their trials, yet allowed them to maintain such phenomenal dynamism? When they were just disciples, that was not how they had been. They simply followed Jesus, as He served His Heavenly Father by doing His will at all times.

Even with Jesus beside them they were often hesitant, sometimes quarrelsome, mostly ineffective and inarticulate. Talking about their being ineffective, we only have to recall when their Leader, Jesus was taken by the soldiers and put on trial. The record shows that they ran into hiding and those who were questioned about their relationship with Him denied ever knowing Him. They were not even loyal, were they? And the people around them, those who listened and watched curiously, were no better.

There was a real dearth of spiritual perception. Therefore Jesus went to the Cross as one of the loneliest and most misunderstood men in all history. Yet those disciples and many others who followed Him then, and had proven to be such miserable failures, were destined to be not only His protégés, but His champions.

After Calvary they were deprived of His physical presence. They could no longer tread those dusty roads with Him. They were at their wits end as to how they would manage. This is made clear when we consider the two who were on their way to Emmaus (Luke 24:17). They were obviously discussing how horribly He had suffered and died on the cross at the hands of cruel men, when suddenly the risen Saviour presented Himself, and joined them in conversation. As if He didn't know, He asked them, *'What manner of communications are these that ye have with one another, as ye walk and are sad?'*

It is significant that they did not even know Him, the man with whom they had been for years. In fairness to them though this was the risen Christ. No one so far had known Him in resurrection. The Bible says, *'Their eyes were holden that they should not know Him.'*

They even asked Him whether He was a stranger and did not know about the horrible crucifixion that had recently taken place. They bemoaned the death, the cruelty of it all, and how their hopes had been dashed, for they had been looking to the man as the one who was going to 'redeem Israel.' When they had finished speaking Jesus took the opportunity of putting the record straight. He told them that they were not in the proper state for realizing all that had happened, for they were still in unbelief. *'Ought not Christ to have suffered these things, and to enter into His glory?'* He asked them: *'And beginning at Moses and all the prophets, He expounded unto them in all the Scriptures the things concerning Himself.'*

This is not to say that the disciples up to this time had not been the Lord's. We must remember that they were not volunteers. It was He who had called them to follow Him, and He had expressly told them in Luke 10:20 that their names are written in Heaven. In John 13:10,11, He even said that they were already clean. Nevertheless, Pentecost was going to clarify beyond all contradiction that they were not only born of the Spirit, but baptized in the Spirit, marked out for service.

Let us not forget that Jesus Himself had earlier had this baptism. After He had been baptized in the river Jordan by John the Baptist, the Spirit descended on Him marking Him out, if for nothing else, for power and ministry. John had forseen this and prophesied, '*I saw the Spirit descending from heaven like a dove, and it abode upon Him. And I knew Him not: but He that sent me to baptize with water, the same said unto me, upon whom thou shalt see the Spirit descending, and remaining on Him, the same is He which baptizeth with the Holy Ghost. And I saw, and bare record that this is the Son of God*'(John 1:32–34).

Jesus having received this baptism, anyone might have thought that He would go straight out into the ministry and start doing mighty supernatural works, but it was not like that. According to the record in Matthew 4, '*He was led up into the wilderness to be tempted of the Devil.*'

That was amazing! Just think of it! God allowed the Devil to tempt Jesus, and at such a critical time. If He was tempted on receiving the baptism in the

Holy Spirit, what about us when we receive? As we receive, we also begin to realize that we now possess the basic essentials for Christian life and ministry. It is then that we start to appreciate that there is a goal in view, *'The measure of the stature of the fullness of Christ.'* That is it, if we are going to serve as He did. We must be equipped. We must be empowered from on High, as He was, that we may pray as He prayed; that we may speak as He spoke. He did not beat the air. When He spoke it was Spirit and Life, always effective. It is obvious He did not expect us to be insignificant. He said we are the salt of the earth. In other words we are preventing the earth from rotting. If we were suddenly taken from the earth the whole place would be overcome with evil. That is certainly not God's plan.

Safe From Shipwreck

Our presence here is essential to Him. Look at Isaiah 42. It gives a clear picture of how God sees His anointed ones, those who are 'standing in the gap;' – or to use a slightly different analogy, those who are equipped to occupy till Jesus comes. *'Behold my servant, whom I uphold; mine elect, in whom my soul delighteth; I have put my Spirit upon Him: He shall bring forth judgement to the Gentiles. He shall not cry, nor lift up, nor cause His voice to be heard in the street . . .'* Essentially this speaks of Jesus in His role as Servant. It is God's testimony as to the Person in whom He finds the greatest of pleasure. None of us can arrive at that calibre of manhood by our own efforts, nor by education, Bible college training or devotion to Christian ethics; as we have been seeing, it must be that He has put His Spirit upon us. Then and only then can we display His nature and do His will.

Is it not amazing that God chooses the most unlikely persons to do His work? And you can see why, can't you? His work requires His Spirit, His power, His anointing that all the credit might be His.

The Bible makes it clear that it is *'by the anointing the yoke shall be destroyed.'* Without it you cannot do anything supernatural. You cannot heal the sick, you cannot cast out demons, raise the dead, speak words of Spirit and of Life, or successfully point a sinner to the way of Salvation. You cannot praise the Lord as you ought. The list of 'cannots' is endless. It must be for this reason why the message of Isaiah 42 is so compelling. That 'Behold' with which the chapter commences speaks volumes. There are thousands today under the yoke of bondage. They are bound by sin, sickness and disease. Their hearts are racked with pain and suffering. Where is the solution? Not a million miles away. You are that solution! Your being available to God for the anointing to operate in and through you is a tremendous link in the chain of events that shall lead up to *'the knowledge of the glory of the Lord'* filling the whole earth, *'as the waters cover the sea'* (Hab. 2:14). What God says in Haggai is very pertinent to this: *'I will fill this house with glory . . . the glory of this latter house shall be greater than of the former, saith the Lord of Hosts: and in this place will I give peace, saith the Lord of Hosts'* (Hag. 2:7,9).

Of what house could He be speaking but His people? He will fill us, *'the habitation of God through the Spirit,'* and the splendour of His house shall be incomparable in us all over the earth. That will be something to behold! So Isaiah 42 is very comprehensive, speaking so strikingly of our Saviour who in partnership with God the Father was the very originator of this Divine plan of Salvation.

Christ is supremely God's delight. God sits today as the great refiner of silver, and would bring out the strength of faith and endurance in us that accord with the nature and lifestyle of the Great Servant. Hence *'Behold my Servant whom I uphold: mine elect, in whom my soul delighteth; I have put my spirit upon Him'*(Isa. 42:1).

"That is my servant" God would say, and He loves to bring out these features of Christ in those who are in His service. The Bible speaks of *'Christ in you the hope of Glory.'* God is pleased to test us in the furnace of fire, as this produces endurance, the Divine nature working in us, which is so fragrant to Him. This principle is seen in Daniel, regarding Shadrack, Meshack and Abednego in the furnace. Their names appearing several times in the chapter is clear evidence of the pleasure God found in them. And there was a fourth person walking with them in the furnace heated seven times, and He was like unto the Son of God. What honour, what credit, what distinction! God would put us to like tests often to honour us.

The apostle Paul was tested to the utmost in his long cheerless voyage and here is his comment; *'For there stood by me this night the angel of God, whose I am, and whom I serve, saying, fear not, Paul . . .'* (Acts 27:23). This was Paul's cover, so to speak, in the most trying and difficult circumstances; the angel standing by. That brought him to dominance. He was to be seen as Master of the ship and no one on board 'with him' should suffer any harm. They were all to land safely.

The great challenge to us right now is whether we are really on board the ship with 'The Captain of Salvation.' In other words are we totally with Him in Spirit? Herein lies the secret of a successful landing or acceptable service. How Paul must have prayed for all on board! That was wonderful. He would not have wished for any to be lost. Need one say that was the Spirit of Christ on display in His servant, that caring Spirit we see especially in John 17? Note the soldiers would have selfishly got off the ship during that crisis but the apostle sought the salvation of all. In that attitude his dominance was expressed, the angel of the Lord standing by being his assurance of faith. This principle applies to the local church in conflict. If they will sail with you everyone can and will be saved from shipwreck.

We do well to remember that Paul was so used to the Holy Spirit speaking through him that he had the ability to distinguish between his own thoughts and the Spirit's (1 Cor. 7). When Paul faced judgement at the hands of the King it was soon evident who his friends really were. *'All men forsook me,'* he said, then later, *'the Lord stood with me and strengthened me.'*

Paul was to present his own defence. That was normal, but he was not alone as the onlookers might have thought. The Lord was there, his wonderful support. What blessed assurance in the presence of the 'lion's mouth'! Paul was as calm as ever Shadrack, Meshack and Abednego were in the fiery furnace or as Daniel was in the den of lions. We do not read that the lion's mouths were shut. The Lord did not shut them. No doubt that was deliberate. He could also have shut the mouth of the Emperor; He could at least have stricken him, but He did not. Instead He delivered Paul from him. That was by far the greater thing. It emphasises the majesty of the power that is by the side of those who serve the Lord – power to deliver them in the most extreme situations of opposition or conflict. Those who will stand up for Him, He will stand up for them both to deliver, and finally to give them a triumphal entry into His everlasting Kingdom.

Chapter 8

Holiness Today

'And with great power gave the Apostles witness of the resurrection of the Lord Jesus: and great grace was upon them all.' Chapter 4 of Acts ends on this high note.

Chapter 5 starts with a very serious account of drastic judgement upon a couple of the Church members, Ananias and Sapphira. They had decided to deceive the congregation over the price they had received for a certain property, and being not obliged to tell anyone about either the property or the money, they decided to conceal the full proceeds of the transaction, and present half that sum as the total received.

We cannot be certain as to what was in Ananias' mind in conceiving this trick. Perhaps he thought that he would prove whether the congregation could see through him. On the other hand he might have wanted to impress the Church with his personal generosity in that no doubt his intention was to contribute that half or at least a part of it to the church's funds. However, *'God is not mocked'* says the Scripture. We cannot play fast and loose with Him. In a church such as that Early one was, moving under the anointing and power of the Holy Spirit, it is a very dangerous thing for any avowed

Christian to practise deceit or lying. As we shall see in the case of this particular couple the Holy Ghost wreaked disaster upon them. They did not live to perfect their deception.

On a certain day Ananias went to church about three hours in front of Sapphira, and as was agreed between them he laid the money *'at the Apostles' feet.'* Being full of the Holy Spirit, Peter soon recognised the plot and was quick to expose it. Like many today, up to this time Ananias and his wife did not realise that dealing with the Church is the same as dealing with God. Peter challenged Ananias by asking *'Why hath Satan filled thine heart to lie to the Holy Ghost, and to keep back part of the price of the land? . . . thou hast not lied unto men, but unto God.'* Hardly had Ananias heard those words than he fell to the floor dead. What a lesson that must have been to the congregation, and how much we should learn from this!

The same fate awaited Sapphira. She did not know anything about her husband's death and coming into the church her first contact was Peter. No doubt she appeared as innocent as ever when he asked her whether they had sold the property for such and such a price. She confirmed the deceit by answering yes, whereupon *'Peter said unto her, how is it that ye have agreed together to tempt the Spirit of the Lord? Behold, the feet of them which have buried thy husband are at the door, and shall carry thee out.'*

So Sapphira died just like her husband had done *'And great fear came upon all the church, and upon as many as heard these things.'*

Therefore, the fact that so many in our churches today lie, deceive and do many un-Christian deeds with ease, as it were, not fearing exposure, and even less sudden death, is not due to cleverness. Rather it is an indictment on the Church. Where the Holy Ghost is in charge sin does not persist. Working through Christ's anointed people He will always overthrow the enemy's work. It is a very sobering thought that the Church must be holy. *'Without holiness no man shall see the Lord.'* On an individual basis each person is required to be holy. Holiness is of the Lord. His glory, His presence is upon His Church. We must settle it in our hearts that lying and deceit play no part in holiness.

The tragedy that took place in that church regarding Ananias and Sapphira is of momentous significance. It heralded cleansing, the fear of the Lord, a healthy respect for His ministers, the necessity to be upright in business and emphasised that God will have truth rather than a lie, to mention but a few things. Apart from these, what practical lesson can one learn from this affair? I believe it is a stark and cogent reminder that no Christian wife is obliged to connive with her husband to do wrong, and vice versa. We already know that there are specific injunctions in the Scriptures for wives to be obedient to their own husbands and even to be submissive to them. But that's not all there is to it, as some would have you believe.

Ephesians 5:22 is a clear rendering of the facts. *'Wives, submit yourselves unto your own husbands, as unto the Lord.'* That qualifying clause, *'as unto the*

Lord' really says it all, does it not? It presupposes that the husband is himself already submitted to the Lord. If only Sapphira had objected to the connivance to deceive the Church, she and her husband might have lived on and been a great asset to that congregation.

The brunt of the responsibility was obviously Ananias'. He could, as head of the family, have demanded that she complied with him, but when the crunch came all she needed to do was to have told the truth to the minister, Peter, and the story would have been very different today. It is interesting to read what Jesus said about the wife and husband relationship when the choice has to be made between following Him remaining in a situation of compromise. One record is in Luke 18:29: '*And He said unto them, verily I say unto you, there is no man that hath left house, or parents, or brethren, or wife, or children, for the Kingdom of God's sake, who shall not receive manifold more in this present time, and in the world to come life everlasting.*' According to Jesus there can be no reconciliation between life and death. To follow Him is the way of life, and conversely to neglect following Him is the way of death, eternal death. However much we might love someone, loving Christ takes precedence over that and demands unparalleled standards based upon His Word.

Holiness Cannot Be Earned
We very briefly discussed holiness. That point deserves further comment. Repentance and holiness

go hand in hand and both are gifts from God. I cannot make myself holy. It is the sovereign work of the Holy Spirit upon one's life that makes one holy. God changes us from one degree of Christ's likeness to another, all we have to do is yield; *'According as He hath chosen us in Him before the foundation of the world, that we should be holy and without blame before Him in love . . .'*(Eph. 1:4).

You do not become holy by repentance. Repentance is the key to salvation. But salvation is a big word, a cliché perhaps. What we are really saying is that without repentance we are unable to know God as our Father. Obviously, God is the *'God of all flesh'* (Jer. 32:27), but to us who know and love Him, He is our Father through Jesus Christ. Hence, the Bible says much about repentance. One particular verse comes readily to mind. *'Let the wicked forsake his way, and the unrighteous man his thoughts: and let him return unto the Lord, and He will have mercy upon him; and to our God, for He will abundantly pardon'* (Isa. 55:7). According to this, God is more willing to forgive man than man is willing to repent. Therefore God invites, even pleads with him to receive mercy. God is furnishing His Kingdom with men and women who are repentant. That is the picture that comes into focus when one reads the Gospels. He has a Kingdom here which is not of this world.

For a good example of mercy in operation we have only to reflect on Simon Peter's encounter with Jesus. The record is in Luke 22: *'And the Lord said, Simon, Simon, behold, Satan hath desired to have you, that he may sift you as wheat: but I have prayed for thee, that thy faith fail not: and when thou art converted, strengthen thy brethren.'*

Feeling confident in himself about following Jesus to any length, Peter was unable to accept Jesus' counsel and replied, *'Lord, I am ready to go with thee, both into prison, and to death.'* No doubt Peter meant every word of that, and his resolve was firm. But Jesus could see ahead and knew that he did not possess the power to do all that he had said and replied *'I tell thee, Peter, the cock shall not crow this day, before that thou shalt thrice deny that thou knowest me.'* We must not imagine that Peter was arrogant. Any one of us might have behaved as he did if we were faced with the same set of circumstances. It takes God, and God alone, to keep us from falling.

Note however, Jesus had prayed for Peter. We cannot think of His prayers not being effective. He knew that He was facing the Cross of Calvary. He knew that He would be bearing all the weight of sin and its consequeces for the fallen race of mankind. That was imminent, but He made time to pray for His friends. Verse 41 shows Him withdrawn from them about a stone's throw and kneeling in prayer. What humility! What faith and trust in God that showed!

Soon after that He was arrested. *'Then took they Him, and led Him, and brought Him into the high priest's house. And Peter followed afar off.'* Already Peter is drifting. Will he manage even a semblance of what he said he would do go with Jesus to prison, and death? Not likely. Instead, he was identified with a group of people who sat indifferent to the momentous occasion of the Saviour, an innocent man, being accosted and taken into custody. One young woman looking at Peter as he sat there, accused him of having been with Jesus. *'And he denied Him, saying, woman, I know Him not.'*

Of course, that was the beginning of the fulfilment of Jesus' words. Hardly had that happened when someone else said virtually the same to Peter, as that young woman had done, and again he denied the Lord. Finally a third person confidently affirmed that Peter being a Galilean was one of Jesus' friends, but he continued to vehemently deny that he ever knew Him. Immediately, the cock crowed, and Peter remembering what Jesus had said, went out weeping bitterly. To the unsuspecting, Peter had so badly failed the Lord that he could not ever hope to be identified with Him again, but the grace of the Lord knows no bounds. No one can be too far gone to be reached by it.

One day, soon after, Peter would qualify for singing with the ransomed:

> Grace! Tis a charming sound, harmonious
>   to the ear,
> Heaven with the echo shall resound,
> And all the earth shall hear.
> Saved by grace alone!
> This is all my plea;
> Jesus died for all mankind,
> And Jesus died for me.

Jesus knows our weaknesses as much as He knew Peter's. As we have seen, He knew that Peter would fail, would deny Him, but He loved him the way He loves us, – unconditionally. The Bible says, *'For He hath made Him to be sin for us, who knew no sin; that we might be made the righteousness of God in Him.'* (2 Cor.5:21). In other words, God took all our sin and put them on Christ's account. Then He took all Christ's righteousness and put it on our account. Christ took our failures, diseases and defeat. Now when God looks at us He sees us through Him. All that Jesus is, God has made us to be.

Therefore although we cannot excuse imperfection, we must acknowledge that God uses failures, imperfect, marred vessels to express His glory. I am yet to meet anyone who has never failed. But we must re-emphasize that failure does not disqualify us from receiving mercy. In Luke 6:40, Jesus says *'The disciple is not above his Master: but everyone that is perfect shall be as his master.'* Thanks be to God, His *'free gift is eternal life through Jesus Christ our Lord.'* This is unchangeable. It is on the basis of this gift that we have life like His, eternal life, and are regarded by Him as perfect.

I cannot recall a day in all my many years as a born-again Christian when I have felt particularly holy. Perhaps that state is not one that can be felt, but it is worth emphasizing that as we walk with the Lord and keep short accounts with Him, holiness is attributed to us by Him, *'who,'* according to 2 Timothy 1:9, *'hath saved us, and called us with an holy calling, not according to our works, but according to His own purpose and grace, which was given us in*

Christ Jesus before the world began.' We are therefore unable to boast of being holy, as it is really nothing to do with us. We are not able even to walk with the Lord unless He keeps us. Herein is the mystery of our salvation. Therefore, I am further encouraged as I read a passage such as Leviticus 11:45, *'For I am the Lord that bringeth you up out of the land of Egypt, to be your God: ye shall therefore be holy, for I am holy.'*

It is worth noting that it does not say we 'must' be holy. That would presuppose that we do have the ability to be holy and are consequently expected to be, through effort on our own part. Instead of that God takes the full responsibility for our holiness. So He explains that it is He who has brought us up out of the land of Egypt (the world of the ungodly) to be our God.

Of course, while we were in Egypt we did not know Him. We were strangers, we were foreigners. But now we have a relationship with Him by virtue of what He has done, and therefore shall be holy, for He is holy. And He has declared Himself as the Lord, our God. I do not know about you, but I very much revel in the idea of being brought 'up' and 'out' of the land of Egypt. This certainly signifies a great deliverance which is confirmed in the New Testament *'that we should be saved from our enemies, and from the hand of all that hate us . . . that He would grant unto us, that we being delivered out of the hand of our enemies might serve Him without fear, in holiness and righteousness before Him, all the days of our life'* (Luke 1:71–75).

Chapter 9

666 And the Clamour for Unity

We have clearly seen that God wants us to live holy lives, lives that honour Him. Then, as we continue to grow in our walk with Him, He can prepare us for the unique circumstances facing every Christian as we approach the End-Time.

According to Mark 1:14, Jesus came into Galilee preaching the gospel of the Kingdom of God. That Kingdom about which He was speaking was that of His reign in us. It is really the power and reign of God being set up within us, as His people through whom He functions to reach out, change, lift and restore human beings to fellowship with God, such as He had with Adam and Eve before they fell.

That is Good News. So Jesus told us to repent and believe the gospel. It is difficult for human beings to repent or change their minds about God. They tend to think of Him under the Old Testament concept of law, justice, judgement, retribution and suffering – of chastisement, punishment, penalty and legality. But He is not like that. As revealed in Christ, He is the God of all grace, of compassion, love and purity. His eyes, says Hab. 1:13 are *'purer eyes than to behold evil.'* He cannot look on iniquity. Hence He has created you in Christ *'that ye may be blameless and harmless, the sons of God, without rebuke, in the midst of a crooked and perverse nation, among whom ye shine as lights in the world'* (Phil. 2:15).

Individually then we are enabled to dispel darkness and to make clear the path for others. When the Early Church spoke people took notice. They had to, because what they heard was authoritative and compelling. As lights in a dark world those Christians shone for the pleasure of their God. They gave direction to the lost. Their testimony affected governments and every aspect of society. That is another thing that is so lacking today in our Christian witness, clear and unequivocal direction from us to the government and society.

We manage to stop some laws being ratified. Admittedly some inconvenient ones do get through, but often that is only because we are not as united as we could be. I mean the whole body of Christ. If we are really united, God can move in a way that the world will begin to see that the Church has put herself in proper order, and can therefore speak about the government doing the same.

We have no really Christian voice in the government – just a notional ecclesiastical verbiage. That is not enough. It is not that clear directional light that the Holy Spirit gave through the ministry of the apostles. He needs to speak through us, but He cannot speak through anything but unity, and at present that is just what the Church lacks. As we have seen before, it is not that the government does not have its policies and politics, but what do they matter! They only add to the ever worsening muddle. It is only the Christian Church, the people of the Living God, that can show the Way. As lights, we must shine in this dark world and should be prophesying to the government. We should be accurately predicting future events. These should not be left to presidents, politicians and other 'professional leaders.' It is heartening to hear the media reporting that the President of the U.S.A. consults Billy Graham the well known evangelist for spiritual advice. That is a notable step in the right direction for which we can thank God. It is a positive sign that God's people are prevailing in prayer, and why shouldn't they?

Prayer For Unity?

I was at a most exciting prayer meeting recently which gave me real hope for the future. The people were certainly laying hold of God almost as if it were the last hour. There was a cogent urgency in their cry. They prayed for both the local and central government, that God would raise up men in those high offices of state to give a spiritual lead to the nation. They prayed particularly for the prime minister that he might receive Christ as Saviour and Lord, that our government would soon become a sample for good throughout the world. They also prayed for the Church that it might not be perceived as fragmented, but one in Christ. For me, that was tremendous and warrants some godly applause. Yet when we look at Ephesians 4 there arises an inevitable question as to whether it is of any value praying for unity. Verse 3 encourages us *'to keep the unity of the Spirit in the bond of peace.'*

So God has already given that to us. Unity and peace go hand in hand and cannot be divorced, the one from the other. What good is it then to be asking for what has already been given to us! Practically, it might not be apparent, but a little more submission to God and His Word will make all the difference.

Sometimes through failing to recognise who we really are in Him we do not live up to the standard that is required of us. This is not new. Even King David of old was guilty of this, if guilt is the right word. The time came when he perceived that God had *'confirmed him King over Israel, for his Kingdom was lifted up on high, because of his people Israel'* (1 Chron. 14:2). His was a most exalted Kingdom.

While David remained unaware of what God had done for him, and the mighty person he had miraculously become, by the grace of God, as a warrior he was inactive. But now it had dawned on him that he was a mighty King after all, and that God had promoted him to a special place of dignity and poise. Some of us might think that that being so, his enemies would have respect for him and relent. It was not like that. All of them went to attack him. *'And David heard of it, and went out against them.'* I believe this is a signal lesson to us. David didn't wait to be pounced on by his enemies. He knew that they were on their way and he went to meet them.

It is reasonable to imagine that David could have disguised himself, he might even have run away, but he did not. He was well able to stand his ground for he at last realized who he really was in the sight of God.

'So they came up to Baalperazim, and David smote them there.' Wonderful! He had a tremendous break-through against all his enemies. The record in 1 Chron 14:1 shows him in ecstasy, shouting, *'God hath broken in upon mine enemies by mine hand like the breaking forth of waters . . .'* I believe we should all arrive at our personal and individual Baalperazim/Breakthrough. There the question of unity does not apply, it is more a flowing together in the Lord, appreciating indeed what He has done. Incidentally, in most circumstances the clamour after unity should be viewed with suspicion. Often it is the very basis of humanism, a Christ-less 'togeth-erness' which is nothing less than a forerunner of the Anti-Christ. Let us all beware of a Christless unity.

We have a clear example of this in the EEC (European Economic Community). This is plainly a humanist unification of nations. Since its advent, note how much we are bombarded with the word 'unity' and how far reaching its implications are, touching on every aspect of society, politics, edu-cation, religion, finance, industry, to name a few things. How insidiously this has laid hold on so many, some of whom one would think should know better.

As Christians it is strange if we are not revolted by the recent banding together of certain groups under the title, 'interfaith.' Note the accent here is on unity. But, Ephesians 4 speaks of *'One Lord, one faith, one baptism, one God and Father of all, who is above all, and through all, and in you all.'* Can we improve that? There are not two, three, four . . . faiths.

Unity? – *'The Lord Scattered Them Abroad.'*
In the Bible there is no provision for a rival or equal to Jesus Christ, the Lord. I think above all things God would have us to be single minded about this, lest we be found to be courting disaster. Do you realize that when all these world systems are harmonized they will then be just ready for the dictator, the man of sin, to take over? We already know from the Scriptures that he will eventually; that is inevitable, but we do not have to play into his hands. Paul warns us clearly: *'Come out from among them, and be ye separate, saith the Lord, and touch not the unclean thing; and I will receive you, and will be a Father unto you, and ye shall be my sons and daughters, saith the Lord Almighty.'* (2 Cor. 6:17,18).

Humanism is not a new religion. One of its earliest manifestations occurred at Babel, as recorded in Gen. 11. *'The whole earth was of one language, and of one speech.'* That is how the chapter begins, describing as it does the humanist unity there was at such a time. As one reads one discovers that there is no mention of that confederacy concerning itself with God. Instead, *'They said, go to, let us build us a city and a tower, whose top may reach unto heaven; and let us make us a name . . .'* What ego! What promoting of self! What independence! Could God have tolerated that?

The answer to this question is clearly, no. He did not then, and will not now. It is just a matter of time. Our Saviour Jesus taught, *'Our Father which art in Heaven, hallowed be thy name.'* His is the only name that is hallowed.

We do not want to make ourselves a name to be ultra distinguishable through some Christless humanist unity. God came down and took account of how those united people were doing, making themselves a name, and He was appalled.

There was something else that those people were doing. They were building a city and a tower, whose top may reach heaven. That was the sentiment. What an audacity! They did not mind reaching up to heaven. The top of the tower 'may reach', not that it must or would, but if ever it did it would be a result of their own effort and device.

That tower was indicative of pride in their cleverness, in their technology, such as would allow them to reach up above earth's limitations to the highest place imaginable, and all without any reference to the Almighty. They would be safe and secure in their own unity and arrogance.

As for the city which they were building, that metropolis, that municipality, what could that have been but a caricature of heaven itself? They would rather make their own on earth, anything but that which demands submission to God. Yet as we saw earlier, He is not mocked. He came down and confounded their language and the entire project had to be abandoned. You can imagine when one of the workers asked another for a saw, he received a hammer, and for mortar he was given bricks – utter confusion. *'So the Lord scattered them abroad from thence upon the face of all the earth: and they left off to build the city.'* In that instance God took the initiative against that evil device, and as the Church today seeks to embrace any semblance of humanism the same treatment may be expected.

The Ecumenical movement also has the germs of the unity after which there is this great clamour, unity of faiths, of ideas, of religion, of pursuits. This is obvious to many. The stage is being set for a system of universal religion.

Unity contrived or sought after will culminate in that, and it will not be the cure of all the ills of the world. On the contrary, the man of sin will assume his role as head of such a confederacy, and *'the mark of the Beast,'* as recorded in Rev.13 will be implemented.

To the unsuspecting, the number 666 will then be applied. It will be of common occurrence in their right hand, or in their foreheads. Without this mark none might buy or sell, and there will not be any difference between one country and another in banking and insurance systems, company laws, building societies, speed regulation, commercial practices, medical practice and so on.

Listen to some of the ungodly people today and you will discover that this is exactly what they are working toward, world peace and harmony. Harmony and unity in this sense are married. But even at the expense of boredom we must emphasise that this is a world system, a system devoid of the headship of Christ, against which the wrath of God will eventually be fully expended. When it is mature or fully operational, the coding 666 will be utterly pervasive and privacy such as we know and enjoy today will no longer be. As the man of Sin/The Beast, that genial warm person, which he shall portray, takes up his position he will be in control of many nations. He shall neither regard God nor His Word and shall vehemently blaspheme Him. This is hardly surprising, as his name is 'Anti-Christ,' and the many who shall receive his coding in their body, or who shall worship him, *'shall drink of the wine of the wrath of God . . .'*

This is not meant to frighten us, but rather to prepare us for the imminent future. God does not want us to be caught off guard. Already there are many definite pointers to such a perilous time, The Great Tribulation, as the Scriptures call it.

Nevertheless, on our behalf Jesus has overcome it. This is what He said: *'In the world you shall have tribulation: but be of good cheer; I have overcome the world'* (John 16:33), and again in Matthew 24:21: *'For then shall be great tribulation, such as was not since the beginning of the world to this time, no, nor ever shall be. And except those days should be shortened, there should no flesh be saved: but for the elect's sake those days shall be shortened.'*

So as we saw in an earlier chapter, God has His programme, and He has determined that it must be fulfilled. We shall have to suffer for not taking the mark of the Beast. In fact suffering is a mild description for what many will have to endure. It is

God who shall keep us faithful to the end anyhow, as we yield to Him.

Just cast your mind back as to what we have already said. There shall be no buying or selling without the mark of the Beast. How are the saints going to procure food and clothing? How are they going to manage for transport? Money will be no good to us anymore, perhaps that is just as well; but what about paying our rates or whatever it will then be called? What about paying for our water or lighting? As saints of the Most High we shall be both persecuted and prosecuted, gaoled and ridiculed, but there is nothing to fear for God is on the throne and will never forget His own. In all things He will make a way for us where there seems to be none, and in case we find it too hard and would in time succumb to the entreaty or threat of the wicked one, the Enemy of our souls, God will even shorten the days for us 'the elect.' He will ever be mindful of His people. *'For the rod of the wicked shall not rest upon the lot of the righteous; lest the righteous put forth their hands unto iniquity'* (Psa. 125:3).

Chapter 10

End-Time Power Principles

'*And now, Israel, what doth the Lord thy God require of thee, but to fear the Lord thy God, to walk in all His ways, and to love Him, and to serve the Lord thy God with all thy heart and with all thy soul . . .*' (Deut. 10:12).

Believing God is primary, so is believing His Word. Abraham of old believed God. '*He staggered not at the promise of God through unbelief; but was strong in faith, giving glory to God . . . and therefore it was imputed to him for righteousness.*' God's valuation of him was that, simply because Abraham '*was fully persuaded that, what God had promised, He was able also to perform*' (Rom. 4:20–22).

The Spirit of God is preparing the Church for the return of Christ. Every Christian knows that. Therefore a strong spirit of belief must first come upon God's people that righteousness might prevail. Believing His Word is not optional. It unleashes His power in our lives, power to pray with faith and assurance, power to win precious souls for His Kingdom, power to heal the sick and even to raise the dead. It gives us power with our Maker. Believing His Word is the very strength of our lives. It gives us authority over the very Enemy of our souls. In these the closing days of the Church's history God is seeking for a people who are prepared to live as it were dangerously, one's who will even be fools for Christ's sake. God does not require people to work for Him. That is certain. *'For it is God which worketh in you both to will and do of His good pleasure.'* (Phil. 2:13).

Being filled with His Spirit, as we have already said is of primary importance, then He will work through us. Nor is God seeking volunteers to do His work. For instance, some people have the idea that for a career they can simply go into the ministry, they can enter into clerical orders, as if such would be acceptable to the Lord. On the contrary, He will not have preachers and teachers just because they want to be such. As a matter of fact, currently His work is suffering serious damage through volunteers.

Churches, evangelistic and missionary societies are not required to commission people to the ministry. From Scripture, that responsibility rests with the Holy Spirit. In Acts 13 there is a good example of how the Early Church handled this matter. *'As they ministered to the Lord, and fasted, the Holy Ghost said, separate me Barnabas and Saul for the work whereunto I have called them.'* It is worthy of note that these men were already ministering to the Lord. 'Already' is the operative word. It is a cardinal principle in the New Testament that the Holy Ghost alone commissioned such people. And in our day if He is not the Commissioner we are only adding to the confused state of things generally. That is not what God requires.

The people through whom He works are conscripts, those who can say within their hearts or publicly, *'The Spirit of the Lord God is upon me; because the Lord has sent me . . .'* What the Lord really requires of us today, in a word, is maturity. He is not returning for an immature Church.

Right now God is longing to communicate His thoughts to a people who are, spiritually speaking, weaned from those things that belong to growing children. Isaiah 28 is very clear on this. *'Whom shall He teach knowledge? and whom shall He make to understand doctrine? them that are weaned from the milk, and drawn from the breasts.'* It is obvious that He is seeking a people whose ears are attuned to heaven, a people who can receive His instructions and act upon them. Growth and development of His work in us are the chief characteristics evidenced in that chapter. *'For,'* says He, *'precept must be upon precept, precept upon precept; line upon line, line upon line; here a little, and there a little: for with stammering lips and another tongue will He speak to this people . . .'.*

So God wants to teach us not only knowledge, but also to understand doctrine. Perhaps we should ask why? He reserves the right to put responsibility upon His well developed saints, a people who can handle His business skilfully, who are spiritually mature. *'But there is a spirit in man: and the inspiration of the Almighty giveth them understanding'* (Job 32:8). Is not this verse encouraging?

As to our understanding doctrine, this must be high on God's agenda, considering what Jesus said in John 7:16: *'My doctrine is not mine, but His that sent me.'*

So, much is involved in being sent. God would send us out even as He sent Jesus, equipped with knowledge and a full understanding of our 'doctrine,' to communicate His wonderful plan of salvation to a world that is at ease in sin, and sin's pleasures. He would do this not through a people who are confident in themselves, in their religious knowledge, scholarship or achievements, but by His Spirit. Hence He speaks of them as possessing stammering lips, and another tongue; a dependent people.

Does this mean that you must speak in tongues, as did the apostles and many others ever since Pentecost. Well, why not? If that was good enough for the apostles it must be good enough for us, but that is not necessarily the emphasis here. I believe the Scripture is declaring that you will speak in a manner which is not natural to you. After all, it is a spiritual work. We would expect to be utterly surrendered to the Lord, then what He does in and through us is His prerogative. The main thing is that God wants us to be effective communicators of His grace. Therefore when He says to us *'This is the rest where with ye may cause the weary to rest; and this is the refreshing'* we will act without hesitation or any sense of wavering.

Are Our Hands Too Full?
But the accent is not now on evangelism, healing, deliverance . . . At this time the Lord requires

fellowship, and where can He find this? He wants to pour His love and power into all who will minister to Him personally. He would even have us be His confidant. Isa. 40:31 is of great encouragement on this line, saying as it does, *'But they that wait upon the Lord shall renew their strength; they shall mount up with wings as eagles; they shall run, and not be weary; and they shall walk, and not faint.'* What a difference waiting on Him makes!

Not many of us can draw near to God in the Holy of Holies. However much we hate being alone, when it comes to drawing aside for an hour or so to talk with Him it is more than many seem to be able to bear. Yet it is the only way we can actually minister to Him and be really effective in ministry to the house of God, His people. It is also the only way we can get to know Him well. We have to be violent in our attitude to lay hold of this. The trouble is that so many legitimate demands are foisted upon us. Our hands are full, and there is little or no time to enjoy the quiet, or not so quiet, reading of the Bible and prayer; conversation with God our Saviour.

It is not without significance that the Bible teaches that God requires us to draw near to Him, and He will draw near to us. What is a most fearful thing is that you or I may go out and evangelise, and even win many souls to Christ without any ministry to the Lord Himself. We can be so full of activity based on spiritual principles, and yet be serving the flesh rather than ministering to God's needs. We must always be conscious of this possibility, for God will bless His Word in spite of imperfection in the one who ministers it. Therefore in the final analysis the success of our ministry does not merely depend on us but upon His Word. For *'some indeed preach Christ even of envy and strife . . .'* according to Paul. How pathetic though! Ministry to the Lord does not have to be like that. You can always preach Christ and be blessed yourself in so doing.

Ministering to people by preaching to them should be a natural outflow from ministry to the Lord, and it is certain that you cannot do this to Him unless you are in accord with His Word.

Ezekiel 44:15,16 is a good reference as to serving the Lord in this special way. It shows clearly that God desires something special of us. *'They shall come near to me to minister unto me, and they shall stand before me to offer unto me the fat and the blood, saith the Lord God.'* If we are still in doubt as to what ministering to the Lord really is, perhaps a fuller rendering of our text will further help. *'But the priests the Levites, the sons of Zadok, that kept the charge of my sanctuary when the children of Israel went astray from me, they shall come near to me to minister unto me.'* Without understanding this verse it is easy to be found doing what God has not required, and even acting in rebellion against Him.

On the other hand standing before Him in service is an act of obedience, affording Him much pleasure, as you are not inclining to move until He says you might. Offering the blood, our standing there in front of God is important too. It is the requirement of holiness and righteousness. What is involved in offering Him the fat and the blood? In that we cannot do this literally, what does this mean? Without the shedding of blood there is no remission of our sins: Hebrews 9:22 makes that clear. The blood of Jesus has been shed once for all. By faith we have appropriated that and as we stand before God He acknowledges that fact. To Him then the shed blood is the answer to the demands of His holiness and righteousness, while the fat is suggestive of His satisfaction. The blood has cleansed away all that belonged to the old order of things and the fat ushered in the new. This is best understood in the light of Isa. 53:12: *'Because He hath poured out His soul unto death . . .'* He poured out all of man's life, such as he had by natural birth. Then He was raised up and quickened by the Spirit to live unto God's satisfaction eternally.

So God now requires ministry from us to Himself, but this type of service is limited to a certain place: *'They shall enter into my sanctuary, and they shall come near to my table, to minister unto me, and they shall keep my charge.'* Ministry of this kind is very personal and not public, it is 'unto Me' in the hidden place, the inner sanctuary.

Whilst we are considering the subject of the sanctuary, it is worth noting the garments worn during this priestly service unto the Lord. *'They shall be clothed with linen garments; and no wool shall come upon them, whiles they minister in the gates of the inner court, and within. They shall have linen bonnets upon their heads, and shall have linen breaches upon their loins; they shall not gird themselves with anything that causeth sweat.'*

Of course, for the Christian ministering to the Lord it is not a toil involving sweat. The wearing of linen speaks of the Holy Spirit being upon us. His presence and power with us are the guarantee that we are offering spiritual gifts unto the Lord.

An unspiritual man can only minister unspiritual things. That which is of himself will appear rather than what is of God. It may be the product of a 'graven image' which cannot correspond to Divine speaking or requirements. For instance, often great pains are taken to make what is called the service of God attractive or impressive. But who is impressed? – not God. There might be beautiful musical intonations, religious vestments, and even ecclesiastical jargon; but who is served – who is blessed by these things – God or man? They might please the eye or ear, but only what is of the Spirit will please God. He is jealous over His people, not over the world. He is jealous over all who make a definite commitment to Him.

This is confirmed in Jer. 2:2 *'I remember thee, the kindness of thy youth, the love of thine espousals, when thou wentest after me in the wilderness, in a land that was not sown.'* If you have given Him your affection He never casts it aside, and should it happen that you withdraw from Him, that stirs up His Holy jealousy. Remember love is strong as death says the Bible, and that being so it has its counterpart in jealousy. According to Solomon's Song 8:6: *'Jealousy is cruel as the grave: the coals thereof are coals of fire, which has a most vehement flame.'* What is that, if it is not hell? Happily, that is not our destiny, *'for the love of Christ constraineth us . . .* (2 Cor. 5:14).

'The Yoke Shall Be Destroyed'

The work that God has done in us through Christ is permanent, and He is not finished with any of us yet. Even if we fail He is faithful. His mercies are everlasting, *'For He knoweth our frame; He remembereth that we are dust.'* He is bent on restoring us to that place of dignity and poise in Christ. When the Holy Ghost came upon the disciples they had one objective, that of witnessing to Christ. He had told them this would happen to them (Acts 1:8). That settled it. Afterwards God fitted things into place. It soon became obvious that man's purpose is not just coming to Christ. God requires that he finds a place in the Body of Christ where he can minister, add to the Church and receive ministry. But that is not all. He must be engaged in preparing for His Saviour's return. That being so one's life must be one of conflict and not compromise. Believing God's Word confirms this. The Church also must come into this realisation. This challenge weighs heavily upon everyone who awaits the unfolding of the great and terrible Day of the Lord. At that time many will be judged and found wanting. Today's men of might and power, strong men, men who have enjoyed this world's honour and admiration and all who neglect God will be judged while the remnant will be kept at ease with peace and the joy of the Lord in their hearts.

The entire world without Christ stands condemned whilst the whole world in Him stands forgiven. We have a mandate from God to repel Satan. That among other things is what God requires from us today. That is the task for which He wishes to equip us! It is not His will that any should perish, hence as co-workers with Him we have a message of Salvation in the name of Jesus to everyone who will hearken. God is challenging the Church today to faithfully deliver this message.

It is incumbent upon us to warn people, like John the Baptist did, to flee from the wrath to come. There is a Spirit of faith, a live and dynamic faith in us, which will accomplish this work! The miracle of the gospel that we preach is that through the sacrifice of Jesus mankind can be restored to God, and put back on His level so that we can fellowship with Him. Paul said in Phil. 2:5 that we should let this mind be in us, *'Which was also in Christ Jesus: who, being in the form of God, thought it not robbery to be equal with God.'* The wonder is that we are restored to God in Christ, and there is coming a move of God through the Spirit, in these days which will change society and the way many of us are thinking.

Doctors, lawyers, politicians, psychiatrists, the judicial system and educators do not have the last word. 2 Cor. 2:14 says, 'Now thanks be unto God, which always causes us to triumph in Christ . . .' He is the One we are presenting as the antidote to the worlds ills; the soon coming King of Kings and Lord of Lords.

We cannot force people to believe the gospel. We cannot naturally compel them to receive Christ as Saviour. They are yoked to the enemy by sin. He holds them in captivity to his interests. But what do the Scriptures say in regard to this? *'And it shall come to pass in that day, that his burden* (his yoke) *shall be taken away from off thy shoulder, and his yoke from off thy neck, and the yoke shall be destroyed because of the anointing'* (Isa. 10:27).

The seed of Abraham must be set free from sin's ties to come into the enjoyment of Salvation in Christ the Lord. So God expects us to be anointed with that irrefutable power from on high to effect the final harvest of souls. We ought to thank Him that Jesus Christ the Captain of our Salvation, according to the many infallible proofs of Scripture, *'when He ascended up on high, He led Captivity captive . . .'* The very one who led countless individuals into bondage is now subject to the resurrected Lord of Glory and His anointed saints. That is the truth which the Holy Spirit would communicate to our hearts at this present time that we might really understand who we are in God.

It is dangerous to just muddle along. There is more than that to living in these last days of time. In the Bible we read of the elders of Israel who came together to make David King over Israel. His only credentials for that lofty estate was the anointing. That was his third time of receiving this heavenly endowment.

David was anointed in his father's house and then as King over Judah and here he was anointed King over his own people. Psa. 89:20 says, '*I have found David my servant; with holy oil have I anointed him: with whom my hand shall be established: mine arm also shall strengthen him. The enemy shall not exact upon him; nor the son of wickedness afflict him.*' What a difference this made to David. It was the very presence and power of God with him and upon him, and now he was more than able for the enemy. David had fully arrived at the immutability of his standing in God. It just goes to show that if God's Spirit is upon us we should be attacking the enemy, rather than waiting for his onslaughts, for we know that we are on the victory side.

We already know that the end-time will bring with it times of testing and trial, but as we seek God, listen to His voice and take time to feed our inner man on the powerful sustenance of His Word, we need fear nothing! God has given us the equipment, set out the battle plan, and you and I have the privilege of looking forward to an eternal celebration of a victory that was never in doubt.

Chapter 11

The Giving Heart

As we look forward with growing expectation and excitement to the culmination of God's plan for the ages, there is one vital part of our relationship with Him that we must be particularly concerned not to neglect. Even as the world grows greedier and more self-centered, God wants you and me to turn our hearts outward. He wants us to experience the joy and the spiritual power that accompany a giving heart. God is the author of giving. He so *'loved the world that He gave His only begotten Son, so that whoever believes in Him shall not perish, but have everlasting life'* (John 3:16 Ampl.).

God really gave all that He had, His only begotten, 'only' being the operative word. He gave unstintingly, that we might have life like His, everlasting, once we receive Christ by faith into our hearts. Countless numbers have availed themselves of the virtues enshrined in this text, and have found unparalleled joy and eternal satisfaction in the Saviour. What an investment on God's part that was, and what an exceptional example to us! He gave His one and only, and as a result how many has He today? one million, two million, three million? – indeed an innumerable company.

When we think of all those who have gone on before, having finished their earthly course with manifest love in their hearts for the Saviour, and the vast number who currently are genuine born again Christians destined for heaven, it is phenomenal. For most of us though, as soon as we hear the words give or giving we are apt to think of money. But why should this be so? There are so many other things that can and are being given to this one and that. Giving is really a 'big' word, so much so that it is interrelated with living. Some aspects of giving are abstract, whilst others are tangible. We give encouragement, we give presents, we give thanks, time, gratuity, donation, contribution, grant, offering, consent – the list is really quite long, perhaps inexhaustible, and to every giving there is a receiving. What is more, all this comes from God.

Humbling though it might seem, John 3:27 shows that *'a man can receive nothing, except it be given him from heaven.'* Conversely, none of us has anything to give that we had not first received from God. *'For God giveth to a man that is good in his sight wisdom, and knowledge, and joy: but to the sinner he giveth travail, to gather and to heap up, that he may give to him that is good before God . . .'* (Eccl. 2:26). That practically sums up giving for the Christian.

As we read and believe God's Word our lives are constantly undergoing change. We are bound to recognise that we cannot with too firm a grip hold on to anything that we have in this world, for really, we are no more than stewards. And if we happen to visit a burial ground, lose a loved one or even witness a funeral procession, how confirming these can and should be to us that there is a day of reckoning for all, both givers and receivers.

Father Abraham was a wise man. No doubt he held these thoughts very dearly. We only have to check on his lifestyle once God had spoken to him about leaving his home and family and going out to a land that He would show him. It was one of utter faith and trust in the Almighty. Abraham had certain problems, family ones like many of us sometimes have. Genesis 13 shows that his nephew Lot tried to raise a quarrel with him over grazing land purporting that there was not enough for both of them, and as a consequence their respective servants were always in disagreement. Basically Lot was demanding more land. He felt, and probably quite justifiably, that his cattle had increased beyond or above being maintained on the amount of land that had been apportioned him. That might have been alright, but his attitude certainly was not. It was one of self-justification and contention.

'And Abraham said unto Lot, let there be no strife, I pray thee, between me and thee, and between my herdmen and thy herdmen; for we be brethren. Is not the whole land before thee? Separate thyself, I pray thee, from me: if thou wilt take the left hand, then I will go to the right; or if thou depart to the right hand, then I will go to the left' (Gen. 13:8,9). How beautifully Abraham's decision accords with what Jesus says in Matt. 5:9: *'Blessed are the peacemakers: for they shall be called the children of God.'* This man was pursuing the way of blessing. How much attitudes really do

matter! There is such a clear contrast between these two men, the one being spiritual and the other not.

Perhaps it is time for us to check on ourselves, as to where we stand spiritually. A genuinely spiritual person cannot be mean or selfish and will always be more interested in giving than receiving. Abraham gave up all that people would generally call his legitimate rights to his own land in order to maintain that brotherly relationship, as it says in Hebrews 13:1, *'Let brotherly love continue.'*

Standing Up For Our Rights?

Some of us might think it was made very easy for Lot to love Abraham, as he was given the privilege of choosing any part of the land and as much as he liked. That is doubtful. It does not appear that Lot was in any way concerned about love and affection. The unspiritual man does not think that way. He is more concerned about material gain. Above all things he is interested in making a way for himself. This account of Abraham and Lot should be read over and over again by every serious minded Christian. Verse 10 shows that *'Lot lifted up his eyes, and beheld all the plain of Jordan, that it was well watered everywhere, . . . even as the garden of the Lord . . .'*

That was the start of this man's downfall, although it was not apparent. Blinded by greed, and lacking in vision, spiritual vision, he conceived that that was the place for him to go and make his fortune. God save us from spiritual suicide. It is cruel, it is merciless, it is the result of arrogance and pride.

If only Lot had sought the Lord's pleasure in his

move, if only he had considered the importance of God being consulted first regarding what he was about to do, he might have saved himself and many others much trouble. Remember, the Bible says he *'lifted up his eyes.'* Be that as it may, before long he moved his entire possessions down to the plain of Jordan, the well watered, beautiful pasture land that he had seen close to Sodom and Gomorrah.

What Lot did not consider was that the men of those places *'were wicked and sinners before the Lord exceedingly.'* He little realised the danger of being involved with them and that he might be ensnared in their ungodly ways. Of course, a man in his particular state would normally be sure of himself and even be considered wise by this world's standards. So, *'Abraham dwelled in the land of Caanan, and Lot dwelled in the cities of the plain, and pitched his tent toward Sodom.'* That in itself was grossly unwise on Lot's part, pitching his tent towards sin.

Abraham, as we have seen gave away everything that natural man craves. For the sake of peace he was satisfied to occupy the land that Lot refused. But what was refusal to the one was a fountain of blessing to the other. By his way of living Abraham illustrated the fact that we do not have any rights here. We cannot beneficially lay claims to anything that God has not specifically given us. That is the point of this account. For it was the Lord who *'said unto Abraham, after that Lot was separated from him, lift up now thine eyes, and look from the place where thou art northward, and southward, and eastward, and westward: for all the land which thou seest, to thee will I give it, and thy seed for ever.'* The giver was now the receiver, and note the scale of his receiving – unlimited.

We can afford to leave things to God. True promotion comes only from Him anyway. It does not come *'from the east, nor from the west, nor from the south. But God is judge: he putteth down one, and setteth up another'* (Psalm 75:6,7).

Giving and farming have much in common. It is a matter of sowing and reaping. Every farmer knows that if he sows sparingly he shall *'reap also sparingly,'* but if he sows bountifully he *'shall reap also bountifully.'* That is a fact of life. Referring to Abraham again as our example he certainly sowed bountifully. It is not surprising that he turned out to be one of the richest and most prosperous men of his day.

In the course of time Lot also prospered, but that was not lasting because God was not in it. Lot became identified with the citizens of Sodom and Gomorrah. He learnt their language and their customs, and eventually even became a judge there. But what is more interesting is that but for Abraham's intervention on two specific occasions of momentous crises, he would not have lost just everything for which he had striven, but his very life.

In the first of the two episodes Abraham was able, out of the largeness of his heart, and the prosperity into which God had brought him, to muster three hundred and eighteen of his own trained soldiers to chase after enemy forces and to rescue Lot and his family who had been taken captive. The second crisis occurred when God was about to destroy Sodom and Gomorrah. Abraham pleaded with God for a reprieve for those cities. No doubt his concern was primarily for Lot, and although he did not manage to stay God's hand, as far as the destruction was concerned; all was not lost, for God spared Lot. In a miraculous way there was angelic intervention on his behalf. They '*hastened Lot, saying, arise, take thy wife and thy two daughters, which are here; lest thou be consumed in the iniquity of the city.*'

Many might think that if we had found ourselves in his position we would have welcomed the opportunity of escaping. How we would have gladly hurried out of the impending doom! Lot did not seem even a little worried and simply lingered.

The trouble was that by now he had obviously become so spiritually insensitive that he was not aware of what was really happening. That was the result of how he had lived. '*Be not deceived;*' says Gal. 6:7,8, '*God is not mocked; for whatsoever a man soweth, that shall he also reap. For he that soweth to his flesh shall of the flesh reap corruption; but he that soweth to the Spirit shall of the Spirit reap life everlasting.*'

The angels had to forcibly remove Lot. They '*laid hold upon his hand, and upon the hand of his wife, and upon the hand of his daughters; the Lord being merciful unto him: and they bought him forth, and set him without the city.*' (Gen. 19:16). What mercy God showed him, and with all that, without going into the minute details of the account, Lot lost his wife on the way as they were apparently reluctantly fleeing from the horrendous inferno, when '*the smoke of the country went up as the smoke of a furnace.*' According to the Bible she *'looked back from behind him, and she became a pillar of salt.'*

Was that not a testimony to 'sowing to the flesh' and reaping the consequences? But that was not all, Lot and his daughters escaped the holocaust intact, although only just; and on the way he prevailed upon the angels to let him settle in a place called Zoar because he was apparently too tired to go any further. Later, with his daughters he went up into a mountain and settled with them in a cave. Here, in a moment of wanton indiscretion and unholy stupor brought on by alcoholic drink, Lot committed one of the worst acts of folly that had ever taken place in all the history of Israel. He produced two children by his own daughters. That was most reprehensible.

The Bible says *'Thus were both the daughters of Lot with child by their father. And the first born bare a son, and called his name Moab: the same is the father of the Moabites unto this day. And the younger, she also bare a son, and called his name Benammi: the same is the father of the children of Ammon unto this day.'* Is this not a sad reflection on the mean and quarrelsome, on the one who is keener on receiving than giving? What says Acts 20:35 regarding this matter?' *'It is more blessed to give than to receive.'* Little wonder then that Abraham was so blessed. He believed God and found immense favour with Him. Where others failed he was a thorough success. He was blessed above all, for the Lord even called on him telling him that His covenant is with him, and that he would become the father of many nations. As a model of the faithful he shall never be forgotten.

'And the Scripture was fulfilled which saith, Abraham believed God, and it was imputed unto him for righteousness: and he was called the Friend of God' (James 2:23). Marvellous! Indeed wonderful! If the Bible had said 'a' friend of, that would have called for some elation, but *'the Friend,'* even more so, for it is as though he was the only one. That was how much God must have thought of Abraham.

How To Be At One With Your Message

Of course, he certainly reflected God's giving nature, and God could hardly have ignored that. He never ignores giving on any level. He cannot, for He is its originator. Whenever you discover a spiritual law or principle that the Lord started, you can live in it, live by it, walk by it and always reap the benefits by the Holy Spirit. I contend that there is tremendous blessing to be reaped through giving. All over the Scriptures there are examples of this. One that comes readily to mind is that of the woman of Samaria at the well in Sychar – John 4. It is most interesting when you look into it and realise that Jesus opened up a conversation with her with the expressed desire of bringing her into blessing, through introducing her to the principle of giving. Note He did not go preaching at her. He simply asked her for a drink of water. If she responds favourably she will automatically be involved with Him. Quite naturally, He would thank her and most likely pass the time of day anyway, in that He had put Himself under obligation to her.

I do not know about you, but many are reluctant to involve themselves with strangers. It is so much easier to preach at them, and in this there is a certain detachment being maintained. From the vantage point of the platform, of faith in our message, the Lord Himself, or whatever, we can even tell them that we love them and yet avoid being part of what is on offer in the preaching.

But where is the convincing involvement? Are we ashamed of being identified with our message or the people? Jesus' way with this woman was unique. *'Give me to drink'* He said, blatantly involving Himself with her. Regardless of racial prejudice or suspicion, that was His preferred manner. His being a Jew and her a Samaritan was crucial and bound to cause some reaction, as they were not supposed to have anything in common, but the love of the Lord is not subject to racial considerations.

No doubt wondering whether it was really the drink of water that was most important to Jesus, the woman did exactly what one would have expected of her. She began to talk. That was the very beginning of an eternal relationship, precisely what was intended. For Jesus would almost automatically respond. This was tremendously skillful on His part, was it not? – a wonderful example of personal evangelism, the one to one basis.

She was evidently relaxing a little for she asked *'how is it that thou, being a Jew, askest drink of me, which am a woman of Samaria? for the Jews have no dealings with the Samaritans.'*

You would possibly think Jesus being a foreigner in this area would begin to feel intimidated at least because of the racial barrier mentioned if by nothing else. But no; He targeted her need. It was much greater than His. He would, as it were, ignore her comment and insist on getting down to the heart of the matter before the disciples returned from the shops where they had gone to buy food. So He responded to her by speaking about giving. '*If thou knewest the gift of God, and who it is that saith to thee, give me to drink; thou wouldst have asked of him and he would have given thee living water.*' Was that not tremendous! He introduced His subject so coolly, yet directly and sincerely, speaking of 'living' water. Anybody would want to hear more about that. So the conversation deepened to the point of Jesus being able to tell her convincingly '*Whosoever drinketh of this water shall thirst again: but whosoever drinketh of the water that I shall give him shall never thirst; but the water that I shall give him shall be in him a well of water springing up into everlasting life.*'

This was a very very powerful message, a salvation masterpiece in but a few words. Jesus was simply trying to convince her that once she has received the gift of God it would be an artesian well within her, a constant fount of life, of joy, ever thirst-quenching, ever satisfying. Spiritually speaking the heart of the message was that she could now afford to throw away her buckets. She would no longer be making her way to the well, and no more would she be burdened with the weight of that water from the well on the outside. Marvellous!

Could this woman have refused such an exquisite offer? Could she at this juncture have turned her back on the Giver of Life whose very nature is 'giving'?

By this time she was too far involved for retreating. So compelling was the conversation that there was only one thing she could now say, *'Sir, give me this water, that I thirst not, neither come hither to draw.'*

Perhaps some of us might like to check as to whether we have this well inside, for this is really what Christianity is. Isaiah must have known something about this. In chapter 12:3 he says, *'Therefore with joy shall ye draw water out of the wells of salvation. And in that day shall ye say, praise the Lord, call upon His name . . .'* In what day? When the need arises. God is more and more bringing His people into this realisation. Have you arrived at it?

Throughout this book, we have looked at a number of wonderful, encouraging passages from the Holy Scriptures. We have learned that God has filled His Word with powerful principles that can, if we will apply them, open the way to lives filled with spiritual power and victory. Your life can be a life that affects other lives. Every time you go somewhere, every time you open your mouth to speak in His Name, can be an opportunity for the miraculous. As we approach the closing moments of history, which is after all, 'His Story,' we have the opportunity of doing things that will stand for eternity.

We can be a part of transformed lives, of broken hearts being mended, of healing and help and hope for so many wounded people. The way is clear. The door is open. All you have to do – if you're ready for an outpouring of supernatural Holy Ghost power in your life is – GIVE GOD A CHANCE!